The **JUMBO BOOK** of

SPACE

Text © 2007 Cynthia Pratt Nicolson and Paulette Bourgeois
Illustrations © 2007 Bill Slavin

Compiled from the following books:
Exploring Space © 2000
Comets, Asteroids and Meteorites © 1999
The Planets © 1998
The Stars © 1998
The Earth © 1996
The Moon © 1995
The Sun © 1995

Kids Can Press acknowledges the financial support of the Government of Ontario, through the Ontario Media Development Corporation's Ontario Book Initiative, and the Government of Canada, through the BPIDP, for our publishing activity.

Published in Canada by	Published in the U.S. by
Kids Can Press Ltd.	Kids Can Press Ltd.
29 Birch Avenue	2250 Military Road
Toronto, ON M4V 1E2	Tonawanda, NY 14150

www.kidscanpress.com

Edited by Karen Li and Shana Hayes
Designed by Sherill Chapman

Printed and bound in Singapore

This book is limp sewn with drawn-on cover.

CM PA 07 0 9 8 7 6 5 4 3 2 1

Photo credits

Every reasonable effort has been made to trace ownership of, and give accurate credit to, copyrighted material. Information that would enable the publisher to correct any discrepancies in future editions would be appreciated.

Image produced by F. Hasler, M. Jentoft-Nilsen, H. Pierce, K. Palaniappan and M. Manyin. NASA Goddard Lab for Atmospheres – Data from National Oceanic and Atmospheric Administration (NOAA): page 10. NASA: pages 18, 19, 21, 37, 39, 41 (both), 42, 44 (both), 50, 58, 61, 75 (both), 76, 79, 113, 114, 116, 117, 118 (bottom), 119, 122, 123 (left), 126 (bottom), 128, 129, 130, 131, 137, 139 (bottom), 141, 142, 147, 151, 154, 156, 158 (bottom), 164, 167, 169, 172, 175, 184 (both), 185, 199. NASA, ESA, S. Beckwith (STScl) and the HUDF Team: page 29. NASA/JPL-Caltech: pages 46, 60, 81, 118 (top), 121, 125, 149. NASA Headquarters – GReatest Images of NASA (NASA-HQ-GRIN): pages 62, 86, 196. USGS, J.W. Vallance: page 68. USGS, B. Chouet: page 68. NASA Johnson Space Center – Earth Sciences and Image Analysis (NASA-JSC-ES&IA): page 69. © 2007 Jupiterimages Corporation: pages 71, 89, 92, 94, 96, 98, 99, 102. NASA Kennedy Space Center (NASA-KSC): pages 73, 105. NASA Goddard Space Flight Center (NASA-GSFC): pages 83, 186, 190, 194. NASA Dryden Flight Research Center (NASA-DFRC): page 100. NASA/Jet Propulsion Laboratory (NASA-JPL): pages 106, 112, 123 (right), 126 (top), 158 (top). NASA, ESA, H. Weaver (JHU/APL), A. Stern (SwRI) and the HST Pluto Companion Search Team: page 132. © iStockphoto.com/kickstand: page 139 (top). NASA Marshall Space Flight Center (NASA-MSFC): page 188. Nico Housen and the European Southern Observatory: page 192. NASA/JPL-Caltech/Cornell: page 200.

Library and Archives Canada Cataloguing in Publication

Nicolson, Cynthia Pratt
     The jumbo book of space / written by Cynthia Pratt Nicolson and Paulette Bourgeois ; illustrated by Bill Slavin.

Includes index.

ISBN-13: 978-1-55453-020-5 ISBN-10: 1-55453-020-2

1. Outer space — Juvenile literature.   2. Solar system — Juvenile literature.

I. Bourgeois, Paulette II. Slavin, Bill III. Title.

QB500.22.N518 2007   j520   C2006-902600-9

Kids Can Press is a *lorus*™ Entertainment company

The JUMBO BOOK of SPACE

Written by Cynthia Pratt Nicolson and Paulette Bourgeois
Illustrated by Bill Slavin

KIDS CAN PRESS

Contents

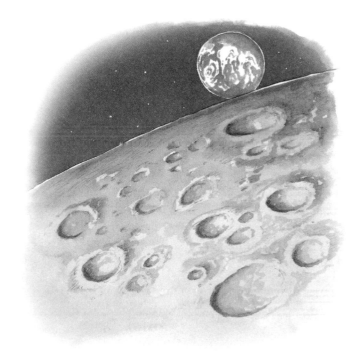

1. Earth: Our home in space

You are an Earthling — you live on planet Earth. People have lived on Earth for thousands of years. Plants and animals have been here even longer. But where did Earth itself come from and when? All over the world people have made up stories to explain how Earth began.

Earth is sometimes called the Blue Planet. Can you see why?

Earth stories

The Hurons of North America said a woman fell from the sky when Earth was covered with water. She had no place to stand. So a turtle swam down to the sea floor and scooped up some mud. The woman patted the mud onto the turtle's back to create the first dry land.

In Mexico, the Aztecs told of two gods who built Earth from a sea serpent's body. When the angry monster lashed its tail, an earth-quake shook the ground.

If you see a word you don't know, look it up in the glossary on page 203.

The ancient Greeks told stories of Mother Earth, named Gaia, who gave birth to the sea and the sky. Gaia's children were gods and goddesses. They made the winds blow and day follow night.

In China, people said everything began with an egg. Phan Ku, the first living creature, hatched from this egg. He carved the mountains and valleys and plains. When Phan Ku died, his bones became rocks. His blood became rivers and oceans. And the fleas in Phan Ku's hair turned into Earth's first people.

How did Earth begin?

Today scientists study the other planets and stars in the universe to find out about Earth's past. Here is what scientists have discovered.

At first, the universe was incredibly hot and everything in it was squeezed close together. Then, about 10 or 15 billion years ago, the universe began to expand and cool. Dust and other particles spread through space. Scientists call this process the Big Bang.

Some of the particles clung together, forming stars and clusters of stars called galaxies. Our Sun was one such star. A flat cloud of dust and gases began to swirl around the Sun. Then, about 4600 million years ago, the cloud separated into lumps. These lumps became the eight major planets, including Earth.

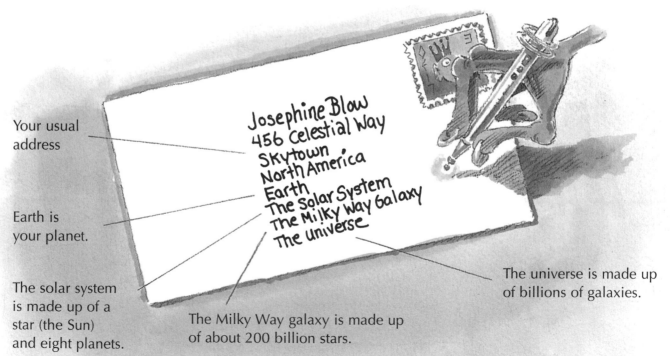

Your usual address

Earth is your planet.

The solar system is made up of a star (the Sun) and eight planets.

Josephine Blow
456 Celestial Way
Skytown
North America
Earth
The Solar System
The Milky Way Galaxy
The Universe

The Milky Way galaxy is made up of about 200 billion stars.

The universe is made up of billions of galaxies.

What was Earth like when it first formed?

If you could travel back to the time when Earth was new, you would find a scorching-hot planet. The atmosphere was thick with deadly gases. Earth's surface flowed with melted rock. There was no oxygen to breathe and no solid land to stand on.

Earth slowly cooled. Its crust hardened. Over time, steamy water vapor in the air changed to rain and filled the first oceans. Living things began to grow in the water. Nothing lived on land for millions of years.

13

What shape is Earth?

Long ago, people thought Earth was flat — like a plate. They worried about falling off its edge. Today we know that Earth is almost round — like a ball. Measurements taken from satellites show that Earth is 43 km (26.7 mi.) thicker through its middle than it is from pole to pole. Like many people, Earth bulges a little around the waist!

The Sun is so big that if it were a hollow ball, it would take 1 000 000 Earths to fill it.

How big is Earth?

Earth measures about 40 000 km (25 000 mi.) around its middle. You would have to fly in a jet plane for more than 30 hours to travel that far.

Compared to some of the other planets, Earth is tiny. Flying around Jupiter in a jet plane would take 14 days.

What is inside Earth?

Scientists have learned a lot about the inside of our planet. By studying earthquakes, they have found out that Earth is filled with rock and metal, which become hotter and hotter toward Earth's center. Scientists have also discovered that Earth's interior has three main layers: the crust, the mantle and the core.

Earth's mantle contains rock so hot that it is slightly soft, like modeling clay.

Earth's core is even hotter. The outer core contains hot liquid rock.

The inner core is solid.

Earth's crust is very thin. If Earth were a tomato, the crust would be its skin.

Earth's crust is like a thin skin of hard rock.

What is Earth's crust like?

Earth's crust is like a jigsaw puzzle made of huge slabs of rock. These slabs, called tectonic plates, float on the melted rock of the mantle below. Ready for a surprise? The tectonic plates are slowly moving. They glide apart, scrape together and smash head-on, causing big changes on Earth's surface. Mountains rise, volcanoes erupt and earthquakes shake the ground.

15

Try It!

Make a hard-boiled model of Earth

YOU WILL NEED

- a hard-boiled egg
- a kitchen knife

1 Gently tap the egg on a table to make cracks all over its shell.

2 Ask an adult to help you cut the egg in half as shown.

The egg white is like Earth's mantle.

The egg yolk is like Earth's core.

The shell is like Earth's crust.

The pieces of the egg's shell are like the tectonic plates that make up Earth's crust.

EARTH FACTS

- Earth orbits the Sun in 365.2 days (one year).

- Earth rotates on its axis in 23 hours and 56 minutes (one day).

- Earth has one Moon, which revolves around the planet every 27.3 days (about one month).

- It takes about eight minutes for sunlight to travel from the Sun to Earth.

- Earth is sometimes called the Blue Planet because water covers three-quarters of its surface. Seen from space, the water makes Earth look blue.

- Thousands of meteoroids hurtle toward Earth every year. Most of them burn up in Earth's atmosphere before they hit the ground.

- Earth is the fifth largest planet in the solar system, after Jupiter, Saturn, Uranus and Neptune.

Jupiter   Saturn   Uranus

Neptune   Earth

What does Earth look like from space?

Only astronauts have been lucky enough to see Earth from space. When astronaut Neil Armstrong looked back at Earth from the Moon in 1969, he was awestruck by what he saw. Armstrong called Earth "a beautiful jewel in space." Blue water and green lands are draped with veils of white clouds. Imagine peering out the window of a spacecraft and seeing this sight. How would you describe Earth?

This photo of Earth was taken by the *Apollo 17* astronauts as they traveled toward the Moon in 1972.

2. Earth, the sky traveler

Are you sitting still? It might feel like it, but you're not. You and Earth are actually hurtling around the Sun at about 106 000 km/h (66 000 m.p.h.). You are breaking the speed limit! Earth's movement around the Sun makes the seasons change. And Earth's turning makes day follow night.

Chasing away the night

Long ago, people thought Earth stayed still and the heavens moved. They made up stories to explain changes in the night sky. Here is how the Vikings explained the movement of the Sun and Moon through the sky.

In the days of trolls and giants, three Viking gods plotted to create a new world. First they made Earth. Then they placed the Sun and Moon in the sky.

But the three gods weren't happy. Nothing moved in their sky! So they put the Sun and Moon into two horse-drawn carts. The Moon was so cold that ice crystals formed in her horses' silvery manes. The Sun made his horses so hot that bellows were needed to cool them.

Trolls who lived on Earth hated the bright light that the Sun and Moon cast in the sky. "Bring back the dark," they grumbled. Two angry trolls came up with a plan. They would turn themselves into wolves and gobble up the Sun and Moon!

The wolves raced into the sky. One chased the Moon and the other took off after the Sun. But the terrified horses pulling the Sun and Moon were too fast for them. Around and around they all raced. As they crossed the sky, night followed day and day followed night. Even now, the Sun and Moon still ride across the sky, fleeing the wolves' snapping jaws.

Why do we have night and day?

We have night and day because Earth turns, like a slowly spinning ball. When the side of the Earth where you live faces the Sun, it is daytime. When your part of the Earth is turned away from the Sun, it is dark and you have night. One complete turn, or rotation, of the Earth takes 24 hours.

The rotation of the Earth makes it seem as if the Sun is moving across the sky. The Sun appears to rise in the east in the morning and set in the west at night. But actually it is Earth that is moving, not the Sun.

It is daytime on this half of Earth

... and nighttime on this half of Earth.

I rotate around an imaginary line called an axis. See how my axis is tilted?

The Sun rises in the eastern part of the sky and sets in the west. At noon, your shadow points north if you are above the equator and south if you are below it.

At sunrise, your part of the world is beginning to face the Sun. At sunset, you are turning away from the Sun.

Try It!

Turn day into night

YOU WILL NEED

- a large ball (such as a beach ball or basketball)
- a small piece of masking tape
- a flashlight

1 Imagine that the ball is Earth. Put the masking tape somewhere on the ball to mark where you live.

2 Go into a dark room. Hold the ball as shown.

3 Ask a friend to shine the flashlight directly at the ball. The flashlight is like the Sun.

4 Slowly turn the ball. Watch the taped spot as the ball turns. What happens?

As Earth (your ball) turns, the place where you live (the taped spot) goes through day and night.

What is Earth's atmosphere?

Earth's atmosphere is a covering of gases that surrounds the planet. Some of the gases protect us from the Sun's harmful rays. Others act like an invisible blanket and hold the Sun's warmth close to Earth.

The atmosphere contains the oxygen we need to breathe. It carries water vapor that falls to Earth as rain and snow. Without the atmosphere, people, plants and animals could not survive.

Exosphere

Thermosphere

Mesosphere

Stratosphere

Troposphere

Why do we have weather?

The Sun heats Earth's surface unevenly. This creates huge blobs of warm and cool air in the lowest layer of the atmosphere. Because the warm air is lighter, it tends to rise. Then cool, heavy air rushes in to take its place. Enormous currents of moving air are produced. They swirl around Earth. The result? Breezes, winds, storms and hurricanes.

Rain and snow fall from the sky when moist, warm air suddenly cools and drops its load of water.

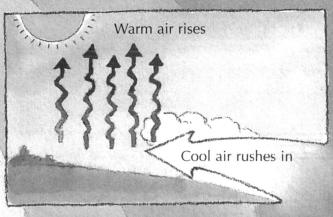

Warm air rises

Cool air rushes in

Try It!

Create some currents

YOU WILL NEED

- a large, wide-necked clear glass or plastic container
  - ice-cold water
  - a piece of string
  - a small glass bottle
  - very hot water
  - a small spoon
  - blue food coloring

1 Fill the large container about two-thirds full with ice-cold water.

2 Tie the string securely around the neck of the small glass bottle. Make a loop you can hold on to.

3 Ask an adult to fill the small bottle with very hot water. Use the spoon to stir in some blue food coloring.

4 Carefully lower the small bottle to the bottom of the large container. Don't let the small bottle tip.

5 Watch for a few minutes. What happens?

The hot water rises because it is lighter than the cold water around it. The currents you have created are like the air currents in the atmosphere that make Earth's weather.

A story about the seasons

In ancient Greek stories, a beautiful goddess named Demeter looked after Earth. She especially loved harvest time, while her daughter, Persephone, loved the flowers of spring.

Below the surface of the Earth lived a god named Hades. His land was dark and gloomy. He kidnapped Persephone because he wanted her brightness to light his world. Demeter missed her daughter so much that she stopped caring for Earth. It began to dry up. Plants died and people were starving.

Demeter told the gods she could not look after Earth until her daughter came home. So Zeus, the father of the heavens, told Hades to return Persephone to her mother. But Zeus had one rule. If Persephone had eaten any food from the underworld, she could not return.

When Demeter saw her daughter again she was so happy that flowers bloomed. Then the sad truth came out. Persephone had eaten four pomegranate seeds while with Hades. She had to go back to him. That meant Earth would die, and Zeus could not bear that. He decided Persephone would live with Hades for four months each year, one month for every seed.

Ever since, Earth is cold and dark while Persephone is away from Demeter. But as soon as she returns, there are spring flowers and sunshine. Mother and daughter spend summer together, but as the time comes for Persephone to leave, plants start to die and Earth gets colder.

Why do we have seasons?

We have winter, spring, summer and fall because Earth is tilted as it orbits, or circles, the Sun. As our planet makes one complete orbit around the Sun, your part of the world is either leaning toward or away from the Sun. In summer, the place where you live tilts toward the Sun. Sunlight hits your area directly, and the days are long and warm. In winter, your part of Earth tilts away from the Sun. Sunlight hits your area at an angle, and the days are shorter. Because of this, you receive less heat. Brrr!

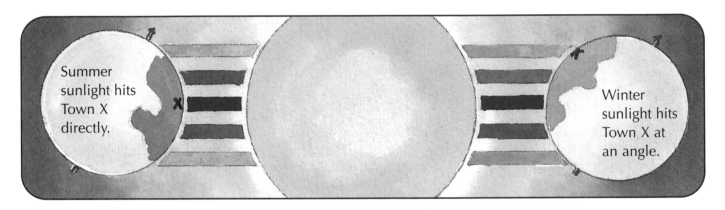

Summer sunlight hits Town X directly.

Winter sunlight hits Town X at an angle.

How far is Earth from the Sun?

Earth is about 150 million km (93 million mi.) from the Sun. Sometimes Earth is a bit closer to the Sun than that. At other times it is farther away. Why? Earth's orbit around the Sun isn't a perfect circle.

Earth takes one year, or 365 days and six hours, to make one orbit. Every four years, those extra hours add up to a whole day, and that day is added to the end of February. This special 366-day year is called a leap year.

Stick your hand into bright sunshine. It took about eight minutes for the sunlight to travel from the Sun to Earth.

How is Earth changing?

Over millions of years our planet has changed in many ways. Once Earth had only one supercontinent. Now it has seven continents — Europe, Asia, Australia, Antarctica, North America, South America and Africa. Even the land itself has changed. New mountains have been pushed up. Old mountains have been worn down by wind and ice and water. The wearing down of land is called erosion.

Earth's climate, which was so warm for the dinosaurs, has cooled. At certain times ice has covered much of the land. Then Earth warmed up again.

Many kinds of plants and animals have appeared and disappeared. During the last 100 000 years, people have spread all over Earth. And with people have come other changes, such as cities and roads and pollution.

Over time, erosion will wear down the jagged new mountains behind me until they look like these rounded old mountains.

What is pollution?

Pollution is anything harmful that people put into the land, air or water. Some pollution from cars and factories rises into the atmosphere. It can eat holes in the layers of gases that protect Earth from the Sun's harmful rays. Or it can make a very thick blanket of gases around Earth that keeps in too much of the Sun's heat. Pollution has changed Earth's climate. And big changes will make it hard for some living things to survive.

Why is Earth a good place to live?

Earth is a special planet. It has just the right combination of warmth, sunlight, water and air for people, plants and animals. Its atmosphere provides us with the oxygen we need to breathe and protects us from most of the Sun's unhealthy rays. As far as we know, Earth is the only planet that isn't too hot or too cold, too dry or too frozen, for the survival of living things.

Astronaut Jim Lovell was part of the first space crew to circle the Moon. When he looked back at Earth, he said, "The Earth from here is a grand oasis in the great vastness of space."

3. Searching from Earth

Space is amazing. It stretches farther than you can imagine and contains more stars than you could ever count. For centuries, people have gazed at the sky and wondered, "What's out there?" Long ago, they told stories to explain what they saw.

The Hubble Space Telescope took this photo of deep space. Each spot of light contains millions of stars.

Early space story

The Cahto people of northern California told this story of how the Sun, Moon and stars came to be in the sky.

One day, Coyote woke up to find the world in complete darkness. The Sun was trapped inside the house of an old woman.

"I must bring light back to the people," said Coyote.

"We will help you," squeaked three mice who were nearby.

Coyote threw a blanket over his head and approached the woman's house. The mice scampered after him.

"I'm a poor, tired traveler," Coyote said to the woman. "Please give me a place to sleep."

Tricked by Coyote's charming voice, the old woman let him in. Coyote began to sing a lullaby and, within moments, the woman was fast asleep. Looking around, Coyote soon found the Sun lying in a corner. It was covered with a blanket and tied down with leather straps.

"We can handle this," said the mice. They gnawed and gnawed until the straps were split apart.

Then Coyote grabbed the Sun. He ran outside and cut the glowing ball into pieces.

Using one leather strap for a slingshot, Coyote flung many tiny pieces of the Sun into the sky. These were the stars. He used a larger chunk to make the Moon. What was left became the Sun we know today. People were overjoyed with the bright and beautiful sky Coyote had created. They showered him with gifts and promised to tell his story forever.

If you see a word you don't know, look it up in the glossary on page 203.

How did people first learn about space?

Early sky watchers tracked the Sun, Moon, stars and the planets visible to the naked eye: Mercury, Venus, Mars, Jupiter and Saturn. People learned to predict the seasons and phases of the Moon. Based on this knowledge, they created calendars.

Although people long ago knew a lot about the sky, they had ideas that were mistaken. Most believed that the Sun and the planets revolved around Earth. Ancient Greeks thought the Sun, Moon, planets and stars were embedded in hollow glass spheres nested one inside the other.

In 1543, a Polish astronomer named Copernicus wrote that all the planets, including Earth, circle the Sun. At the time, very few people believed him.

Where is space?

Space begins about 120 km (75 mi.) above Earth's surface. This is where the atmosphere, a blanket of gases surrounding Earth, becomes very thin. If you could drive a car straight up into the sky at highway speed, you would reach space in less than two hours.

Who invented the telescope?

In 1608, Dutch eyeglass maker Hans Lippershey constructed the first telescope. His basic design — two lenses in a tube — was improved by Galileo Galilei, a scientist in Venice.

With his new telescope, Galileo spotted four moons circling the planet Jupiter. This discovery convinced him that Earth was not the center of the universe. Powerful people of the time were shocked by Galileo's ideas. They confined him to his house for the last years of his life.

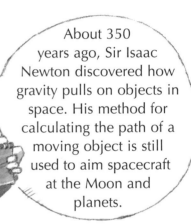

About 350 years ago, Sir Isaac Newton discovered how gravity pulls on objects in space. His method for calculating the path of a moving object is still used to aim spacecraft at the Moon and planets.

How do telescopes work?

Telescopes bend light to make things appear closer. In a refracting telescope, a convex (outward curving) lens focuses light, and the eyepiece lens magnifies the image. In a reflecting telescope, a concave (inward curving) mirror focuses light on a flat mirror that reflects the image to the eyepiece.

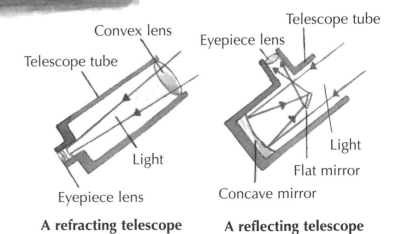

A refracting telescope　　**A reflecting telescope**

Convex lens
Telescope tube
Light
Eyepiece lens

Telescope tube
Eyepiece lens
Light
Flat mirror
Concave mirror

Try It!

Make your own telescope

WARNING: DO NOT use any telescope to look at the Sun.

YOU WILL NEED

- a mirror that curves inward, such as a shaving mirror or a make-up mirror
- a night when the Moon is shining
- a small, flat mirror
- a magnifying glass

1 Point the curved mirror toward the Moon.

2 Move your flat mirror as shown until you see the Moon's light in it.

3 Look in the mirror with your magnifying glass. The Moon should look closer and bigger.

In your telescope, the curved mirror does the same thing your eyes do — it gathers light so you see things. But a mirror can gather much more light than your eyes can. The Moon's light hits the curved mirror so that you see the Moon there. The flat mirror reflects the Moon to the magnifying glass. The magnifying glass makes the Moon seem bigger and closer.

This kind of telescope is called a reflecting telescope.

33

What did telescopes reveal about space?

Telescopes allowed astronomers to peer farther into space than ever before. In 1781, in England, astronomer William Herschel discovered the planet Uranus. In 1846, two astronomers at the Berlin Observatory pointed their telescope toward a spot where others had predicted a new planet would be — and found Neptune.

Telescopes also gave people a new understanding of the stars. By 1923, astronomers had discovered that many spots of light in the sky aren't single stars at all. They are huge groups of stars called galaxies.

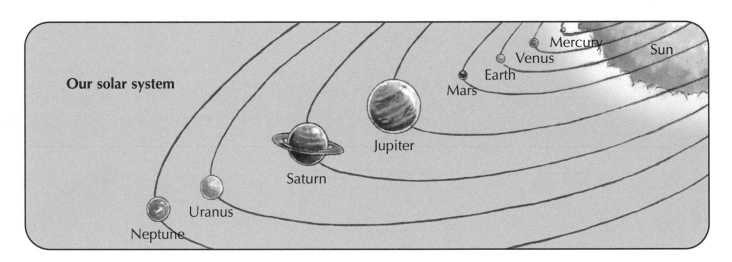

Our solar system

Neptune · Uranus · Saturn · Jupiter · Mars · Earth · Venus · Mercury · Sun

SPACE FACTS

- Some of the earliest recorded sky observations were scratched into clay tablets by the Akkadians, who lived about 4500 years ago in what is now the Middle East.

- Early Polynesians used the stars to guide them on their voyages from island to island in the Pacific Ocean.

- With a strong pair of binoculars, you can see everything Galileo saw with his homemade telescope.

- The first asteroid was discovered in 1801 by an Italian monk named Giuseppe Piazzi.

4. Blasting into space

Have you ever longed to know what's inside a gift-wrapped box? For centuries, people have had that same curiosity about space. Long before the days of rockets and spaceships, people dreamed of zooming into the sky to explore its mysteries.

An ancient astronaut

A daring space flight leads to danger in this Greek myth.

Icarus had been thrown into prison with his father, Daedalus. Escape seemed impossible, until Daedalus had an idea.

"We will fly away from here," he told his young son.

Icarus was astounded, but he helped his father gather feathers from birds that landed on the prison roof. He watched as Daedalus laid the feathers in rows and joined them with drops of melted wax. When the wax had hardened, Daedalus attached the rows of feathers to wooden frames. Soon he had created two sets of enormous wings.

"Strap them on like this," Daedalus said to Icarus. "And slowly flap your arms."

At first, Icarus was too excited, and his wings flapped wildly. Then he learned to control his arm motions. Soon he was flying behind his father.

But Icarus refused to fly steadily. He dipped down to the ocean and soared into the sky. Each time, he rose higher.

"I'm going to touch the Sun!" he called to his father.

"No, Icarus! Come back!" roared Daedalus. But it was too late.

As soon as Icarus went near the Sun, feathers began to drop from his wings. The Sun's heat melted the wax holding his wings together. Without wings, Icarus plunged into the ocean and was never seen again.

When were rockets invented?

Rockets were invented hundreds of years ago in China. They were fueled with gunpowder and used to launch fireworks and weapons. In 1903, Russian scientist Konstantin Tsiolkovsky proposed that rockets be used to explore space. But solid-fuel rockets did not have enough power to soar above Earth's atmosphere.

American scientist Robert Goddard experimented with rocket shapes and fuels, including more powerful liquid fuel. In 1926, he sent the first liquid-fuel rocket a short distance across his aunt's farm. Goddard continued to improve his early designs. His ideas are still used in space-rocket construction.

How do rockets work?

Burning fuel produces hot gases that rush out the back of a rocket and push it forward. Because rockets use so much fuel, they are built in sections, or stages. Each stage falls away after it is used up. This way, a much lighter spacecraft can reach orbit or outer space.

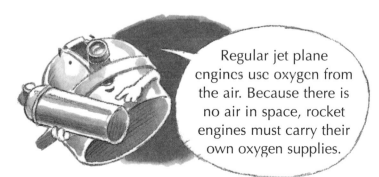

Regular jet plane engines use oxygen from the air. Because there is no air in space, rocket engines must carry their own oxygen supplies.

A *Saturn V* rocket launches *Apollo 11* on its journey to the Moon.

Try It!

Make a two-stage balloon rocket

YOU WILL NEED

- a paper or foam cup
- scissors
- a long balloon
- a round balloon

1 Remove the bottom of the cup with the scissors.

2 Partially blow up the long balloon. Don't tie it closed.

3 Put the open end of the long balloon into the cup and pull it out the bottom. Fold the end over the side of the cup and hold it tightly so air doesn't escape.

4 Push the round balloon up through the bottom of the cup. Leave its open end sticking out the bottom.

5 Blow up the round balloon and squeeze it closed without tying it.

6 To launch your rocket, release the round balloon.

The balloons work like rocket engines, propelling their load forward when gases escape out the back. (The balloons' gas is the air you blew into them.) The round balloon launches the cup like the first stage of a real rocket. When the round balloon is empty, the long balloon takes over, just like a rocket's second stage.

What was the first thing sent into space?

The first object launched into space was *Sputnik 1*, a silvery sphere the size of a large beach ball. *Sputnik* was launched from the former Soviet Union (now Russia) on October 4, 1957. It beeped out a radio signal that was picked up on Earth. This first artificial satellite orbited for 92 days and then fell back into Earth's atmosphere and burned up.

What do satellites do?

Since the 1960s, hundreds of artificial satellites have been launched into orbit. They gather signals from Earth and space and reflect these to collecting dishes on the ground. Using satellite signals, airplane pilots and ship captains can navigate more accurately. Astronomers can learn more about

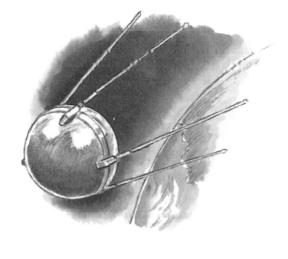

space, and other scientists can track the weather, forest fires or pollution. Satellites also transmit long-distance phone calls and radio programs. Some even deliver the signals for your favorite TV shows.

A satellite is anything that orbits another object in space. The Moon is Earth's natural satellite. *Sputnik* and later human inventions are called artificial satellites.

The space shuttle *Discovery* released this satellite to study Earth's atmosphere.

Try It!

See satellites in the night sky

YOU WILL NEED

- a clear night, just after twilight
- a blanket to lie on

1 Make yourself comfortable staring straight up at the sky. Watch for a tiny starlike dot that takes about a minute to cross the sky above your head. You are looking at a satellite orbiting Earth. (A distant plane will appear to move much more slowly.)

2 Watch for a satellite that gradually fades from view. It is moving from sunlight into Earth's shadow.

3 You may see a satellite that appears to blink on and off as it travels across the sky. You're probably looking at a spinning satellite that has one shiny side and one dark side.

You will see more satellites in summer than in winter. That's because satellites glow when the Sun glints off their shiny surfaces. In summer, your part of the world is tilted toward the Sun. During the first few hours of night, satellites can still catch and reflect the Sun's rays.

Who was the first person in space?

On April 12, 1961, Major Yuri Gagarin of the former Soviet Union became the first human to fly into space. Gagarin's spacecraft, *Vostok 1*, circled Earth once.

In Russia, someone who travels into space is called a cosmonaut. In China, they are called taikonauts.

This is Yuri Gagarin on the day he first flew into space.

In 1957, a Russian dog named Laika became the first living being launched into space. Laika did not survive her journey.

How do astronauts prepare for space?

Astronauts train hard. They exercise every day. As well, they learn all about their spacecraft and any experiments to be done during their mission.

To experience something like near-weightlessness, NASA astronauts put on space suits and enter an enormous water-filled tank. They also take short flights on a special jet that rises, then drops quickly, creating a few seconds of weightlessness. Astronauts call the jet the "Vomit Comet."

Underwater training helps astronauts prepare for space.

41

Why do astronauts feel weightless?

Astronauts float freely in a spacecraft orbiting Earth. So does everything else on board that isn't fastened down. This weightlessness — or "microgravity" — occurs because the spacecraft is continually falling toward Earth at the same time as it is zooming forward. Scientists say microgravity occurs because the spacecraft is in "free fall."

You may briefly feel weightlessness if you're in an elevator that drops rapidly. Do you understand why some astronauts feel sick on their first few days in space?

Tomatoes float above the table as two astronauts prepare lunch in the weightless conditions inside a spacecraft.

What do astronauts wear?

Inside a spacecraft, astronauts wear shirts and pants with many pockets. Outside, they need space suits that provide oxygen, pressure and protection from harmful sunlight. During launch and reentry, astronauts wear "partial pressure" suits, in case of emergency.

The "primary life support system" provides oxygen and pressure. It pumps cooling liquid through plastic tubes in the astronaut's inner suit.

The MMU (manned maneuvering unit) lets the astronaut fly outside the spacecraft. The astronaut can go forward, reverse, turn around and flip over.

A helmet protects the astronaut from micrometeoroids (bits of dust and rock in space) and solar rays. Inside, there is a special cap with a headset.

Steel ball bearings in the suit's joints allow the astronaut to move freely.

The control device lets the astronaut check that the suit is working properly.

Molded gloves protect the astronaut's hands and can be equipped with special tools.

43

What is a space shuttle?

A space shuttle is a reusable spacecraft. It works like a combined spaceship and airplane that carries astronauts into orbit around Earth. (Space shuttles are not used for more distant journeys, such as those to the Moon.) When it lands, the shuttle glides down onto a runway.

With all rockets firing, the shuttle *Discovery* blasts off from the launchpad.

Columbia was the first space shuttle to be launched, in April 1981.

What is a space station?

A space station is a science laboratory in space. The first space station was launched in 1971 by the former Soviet Union. In 1998, several countries began building the International Space Station. Astronauts now live and work in this orbiting lab for months at a time. They perform experiments, observe the Earth and learn how humans can stay healthy in space.

American astronaut Shannon Lucid spent six months on the Russian space station Mir in 1996. Here she floats freely in the station's microgravity environment.

SPACE FACTS

- Alan Shepard was the first American in space. His 15-minute flight in 1961 ended with a splashdown in the Atlantic Ocean.

- In 1962, John Glenn became the first American to orbit Earth. In 1998, at the age of 77, Glenn became the world's oldest astronaut when he flew on the space shuttle *Discovery*.

- Valentina Tereshkova of the former Soviet Union was the first woman in space. She orbited Earth 45 times in 1963.

- On January 28, 1986, less than two minutes after liftoff, the *Challenger* space shuttle exploded, killing all seven astronauts on board.

- Sadly, another seven astronauts died when the space shuttle *Columbia* disintegrated as it reentered Earth's atmosphere on February 1, 2003.

5. Our nearest neighbor: The Moon

What looks bright but makes no light, is a circle one day and nothing at all soon after, looks as soft as cheese but is really hard as rock? The Moon, of course!

Moon stories

Long ago, people explained the riddles of the Moon with stories. In Transylvania people believed the Sun was a king and the Moon was his brother. The Sun married a woman with golden hair and the Moon married a woman with silver hair. Their children were the stars.

The Sun thought the universe was too crowded so he decided to kill his children. But the Moon stopped him. That made the Sun so mad that he started chasing the Moon around the sky — and he's never stopped.

If you see a word you don't know, look it up in the glossary on page 203.

People in Papua New Guinea explained where the Moon came from with this story.

There was only one old woman who knew the secret of fire. Whenever anyone needed fire she went into her hut and brought some out. One day some curious boys waited until the old woman left her hut. They sneaked inside and lifted the lid off a pot in the corner.

The Moon jumped out of the pot and leaped up onto the roof. As the boys followed, it jumped to the top of a coconut tree. One boy grabbed the Moon, but it was so slippery it slid away and flew higher and higher into the sky. It's still there and you can see the boy's fingerprints all over it.

What is the Moon?

The Moon is Earth's satellite and our closest neighbor in space. The Moon is a big rock with mountains, flatlands and craters (large, round holes).

The Moon is twice as big as the planet Pluto!

How does the Moon shine?

The Moon shines with a lot of help from the Sun. The Sun is a star and makes its own light. The Moon makes no light. But sunlight bounces, or reflects, off the Moon. Without the Sun there would be no moonlight.

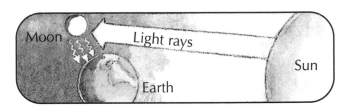

Moon

Light rays

Earth

Sun

MOON FACTS

- The Moon is about 390 000 km (240 000 mi.) away from Earth. If you could walk to the Moon, it would take you almost ten years to get there.

- The Moon is 3500 km (2200 mi.) across, which makes it big enough to cover Australia.

- The Moon weighs 73.5 million trillion t (81 million trillion tn). That's 735 with 17 zeros after it. Earth is 80 times heavier.

- The Moon is over 4.5 billion years old.

Try It!

Find out about the Moon's light

YOU WILL NEED

- a bicycle reflector
- a box or dark room
- flashlight

1 Look at the reflector in the dark room or put it in the box so that no light can reach it. Does the reflector shine?

2 Shine the flashlight on the reflector. Now does it shine?

The reflector shines because it reflects the light of your flashlight. The Moon shines because it reflects the light of the Sun.

49

Is there life on the Moon?

Nothing can live on the Moon. There is no air for plants or animals to breathe. There is no water to drink. When the Moon faces the Sun it is too hot to grow anything. When it faces away from the Sun it is colder than the iciest place on Earth.

This is how the Earth looks from the Moon.

Is there wind or rain on the Moon?

No wind blows and no rain falls on the Moon because the Moon has no air or water. Wind is moving air and rain falls when there is water in the air.

We have air and water on Earth because of the strong pull of Earth's gravity. Gravity is the invisible force that holds everything on Earth. When Earth was forming, gases escaped from its center. But Earth's gravity held these gases close to its surface. These gases became our air, or atmosphere.

The Moon's gravity wasn't strong enough to hold on to any gases that escaped from its core and they floated into space.

Where did the Moon come from?

No one is sure how the Moon formed. But scientists know that Earth and the Moon are about the same age and are made of the same types of rock. Maybe, long ago, when Earth was a hot ball of rock, a small planet hit it. Bubbling rock flew into space, then cooled and hardened to become our Moon.

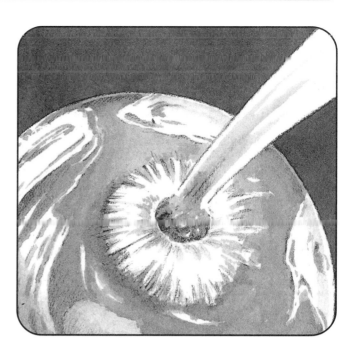

Does the Moon move?

The Moon travels in a path around the Earth called an orbit. It takes almost one month — 27 days and 8 hours — to make one round trip.

You can only see one side of the Moon from Earth. It is called the near side of the Moon. The far side is always hidden from Earth.

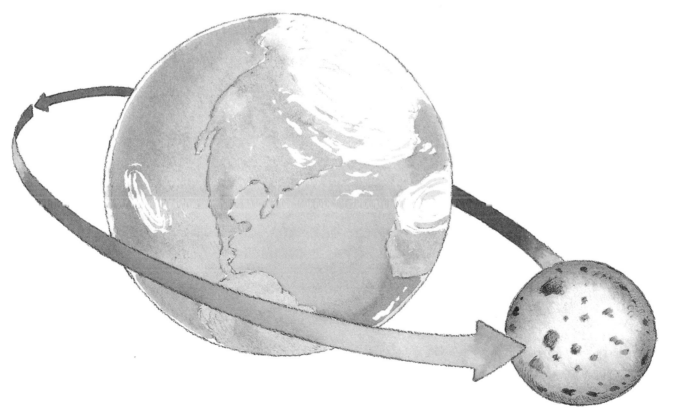

What's on the far side of the Moon?

Until 1959, no one had seen the far side of the Moon. That year, the Soviet probe *Luna 3* took photos of the Moon's hidden face. The photos showed lots of craters, but no large lava flood plains (which form the dark patches we see on the side facing Earth).

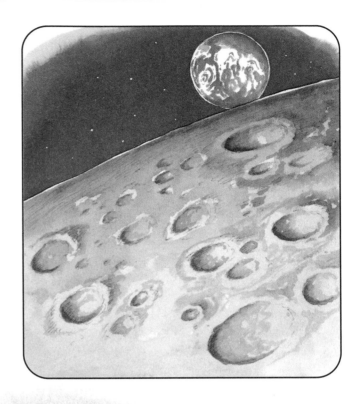

Why does the Moon change shape?

The Moon doesn't change shape. But as it moves around Earth you see only the parts of the Moon that are lit by the Sun. Sometimes you see only a small sliver of Moon lit up and sometimes you see the entire near side.

Each Moon shape you see is called a phase. The phases follow the same pattern every four weeks.

Full Moon

First Quarter

Last Quarter

Crescent

Crescent

New Moon

Try It!

Discover why the Moon has phases

YOU WILL NEED

- a bright desk lamp
- a dark room
- a big, dark-colored ball such as a basketball

1 Pretend the light is the Sun, the ball is the Moon and you are Earth.

2 Stand a little way from the light with the ball in your hands. Hold out your hands so that your arms are straight and the ball is in front of you and a little higher than your eyes. You can see only the near side of the ball. No light shines on it. This is like looking at the New Moon.

3 Keep holding the ball out in front of you. Turn slowly in the same spot, away from the light. You'll see more light shine on the near side of the ball. When your back is to the light, most of the near side of the ball is lit up. This is like looking at the Full Moon.

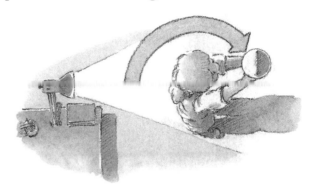

4 Keep turning until you come back to your original position. Did you "see" a Crescent Moon and a Quarter Moon as you turned?

Since the Moon and Earth are always moving, the Sun does not always light the same parts of the Moon. You only see the parts that the sunlight hits.

When does the Moon rise?

The Moon rises at a different time and in a different place each day. The place and time the Moon rises changes because the Moon moves and so does the Earth. You can find out when the Moon rises by checking in a daily newspaper.

In northern countries, the Full Moon closest to September 22 is called the Harvest Moon. For a few days this Moon rises at almost the same time each night — right after the Sun goes down. On clear nights it gives farmers lots of extra light to bring in their crops.

Try It!

Find out why a Full Moon looks bigger when it's low in the sky

YOU WILL NEED

- a Full Moon
- a dime

1 Look at the Moon as it is rising and is near the horizon.

2 Now turn your back to the Moon, bend over and look at the Moon upside down through your legs. Does it look the same size as in step 1?

3 Straighten up and stretch out your arm. Hold your dime up to the Moon. How big is the Moon compared to the coin?

4 Later in the night, when the Moon is higher in the sky, compare it to the dime again. Is it the same size as in step 3?

A Full Moon is always the same size, but your eyes play tricks on you. When you looked at the Moon upside down, you changed the way you saw the Moon and your eyes were no longer tricked. When you compared the Moon to the dime, you proved that the Moon is always the same size, no matter where it is in the sky. Scientists use experiments like this to learn how our eyes and brains judge size and distance.

What is an eclipse of the Moon?

An eclipse of the Moon happens when the Sun, the Earth and the Moon line up in a straight line with the Earth in the middle. The Sun's light shining on Earth makes our planet cast a shadow on the Moon. We don't get a lunar eclipse every month because sometimes the Moon's orbit takes it a little above the Earth and sometimes a little below.

During a lunar eclipse, the Moon can be in the dark for over an hour. But it's never completely blacked out. Sometimes the way the sunlight is scattered and bent by Earth's air makes the Moon red.

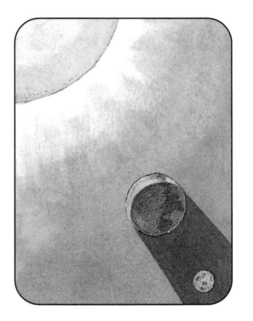

DATE	Where total eclipse will be seen
March 3, 2007	Americas, Europe, Africa, Asia
August 28, 2007	Asia, Australia, Pacific, Americas
February 21, 2008	Pacific, Americas, Europe, Africa
December 21, 2010	Asia, Australia, Pacific, Americas, Europe

A lunar eclipse once saved Christopher Columbus! The explorer and his men were in Jamaica and the native people didn't want to trade any more food with him. So Columbus warned them the Moon would turn red unless they helped him. He knew something the native people didn't — a lunar eclipse would happen that night. When the Moon turned red, the natives thought Columbus had special powers and gave him all the food he wanted.

Try It!

Make an eclipse of the Moon

YOU WILL NEED

- a large sheet of black paper
- tape
- a large flashlight
- a large plastic yogurt lid

1 Tape the black paper to a wall.

2 Shine the flashlight (the Sun) onto the paper. Move the flashlight closer to the paper or farther away until you have a clear circle of bright light (the Moon). Ask a friend to hold the flashlight in this position.

3 Move the plastic lid (the Earth) very slowly and steadily across the beam of light. Watch as its shadow nibbles away at the Moon's image on the paper. You have just made an eclipse of the Moon.

57

6. A closer look at the Moon

Now we can take a closer look at the Moon through binoculars and telescopes. We can see its craters and mountains. But in early times people did not know there were any craters and mountains. They only saw dark and light spots on the Moon. So they made up stories to explain the mystery.

Earth rises on the lunar horizon.

Man in the Moon stories

One Native American tale says a man and his dog are in the face of the Moon.

Another says there is a frog weaving a basket.

A German story says you can see a man with a broom and a woman with a butter churn. Other tales from Malaysia say there isn't a face in the Moon, just a hunchbacked woman fishing with a rat.

Here is a legend from Africa: Long ago the Moon did not shine and it was jealous of the Sun with its bright rays. So one day, when the Sun was on the other side of the Earth, the Moon stole some of its light. The Sun was so mad that it splashed the Moon with mud. You can still see those spots today!

The first person to take a closer look at the Moon through a telescope was the Italian scientist Galileo in 1609. He thought the large dark spots were seas. They're still called that today! Find out more about the Moon's seas on page 64.

Why are there light and dark spots on the Moon?

The dark spots are large, flat areas of dark rock. The light spots are mountainous areas made of lighter colored rock.

If you look at the Moon through a telescope you can see more dark spots caused by shadows of mountains on the Moon. With a telescope you can see other dark spots caused by the high sides of the Moon's craters blocking light from shining into the craters.

The *Galileo* spacecraft took this image of the moon in 1992 on its way to explore Jupiter.

Try It!

Make Moon spots

YOU WILL NEED

- a dark room
- ten small building blocks
- a flashlight

1 In the dark room stand your blocks on a table, leaving spaces between them.

2 Stand back and shine your flashlight on the blocks from about 30 cm (12 in.) away. Look at the shadows the blocks make.

When you shine your flashlight on the blocks, you can see them clearly. That's because the blocks reflect the light. The mountains on the Moon do the same thing, and when you look through a telescope at the Moon you see light spots.

On the far side of the blocks you can see shadows. On the Moon the mountains cast long shadows onto the flatlands. Those shadows are the dark spots you see when you look at the Moon through a telescope.

Mount Hadley

How are craters made?

Craters are deep pits on the surface of the Moon. You can see more than 30 000 Moon craters from Earth. The craters were made when space rocks, called meteorites, hit the Moon. How does that make craters? Imagine throwing a big rock into a sandbox. When the rock lands, sand scatters up and out in a big circle.

That's what happens when a meteorite hits the Moon. Dust and rocks fly up and land in a big circle around the spot where the meteorite hit. That makes the high walls around the crater.

A big city would fit easily in this crater.

Which has more craters, the Moon or Earth?

The Moon has many more craters than Earth. This is not because the Moon is hit by more meteorites. It is because the rain and wind on Earth slowly erase the traces of craters on Earth. On the Moon, a crater can stay the same for millions of years.

Try It!

Make Moon craters

This can be messy. Be sure you have an adult's permission before starting.

YOU WILL NEED

- a deep, unbreakable bowl
- plaster of Paris
- different sizes of pebbles and rocks
- a spray bottle full of water
- gray paint, if you like

1 Pour a thick layer of dry plaster of Paris into your bowl. Hold one of your rocks about 1 m (3 ft.) above the container and let it drop. Do this with all the rocks but try holding them higher or lower above the bowl.

2 Carefully lift out the rocks and pebbles.

3 Gently spray your plaster with water until it is soaked. When it is dry, after about one hour, you can lift your model of the Moon's surface out of the bowl. Paint it gray to make it really look like the Moon, if you like.

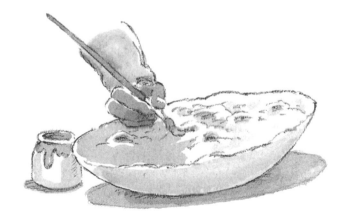

The smallest and shallowest craters were probably made with small rocks you dropped from not very high above the bowl. The heavier the rock and the higher you held it when you dropped it, the bigger the crater.

What are the big, dark spots on the Moon?

Those big, dark spots are wide, flat areas of rock. Some people call them seas, even though there's no water in them. Scientists also call them maria.

Billions of years ago, the Moon was hit by gigantic meteorites that melted vast areas of the Moon. When the melted rock (called lava) cooled, it became the maria.

All of the maria were given names by early astronomers. They have beautiful names, such as the Lake of Dreams and the Sea of Foam. The first astronaut on the Moon landed on the Sea of Tranquility.

From Earth, four of the seas together look like eyes, and a nose and mouth. Look for them next time there's a Full Moon.

Try It!

Focus on the Moon

It takes practice to focus binoculars so you can see clearly with them. Ask an adult to help you.

YOU WILL NEED

- binoculars
- a dark night with a Full Moon
- a pencil
- a piece of paper

1 Focus your binoculars on the Moon.

2 Draw what you see. Can you see mountains, seas and the round rims of the large craters?

You can see a lot more on the Moon when you use binoculars. Use the illustration here to help you fill in some of the details on your drawing. Sometimes when the sky is cloudy or full of pollution, you'll have trouble seeing the Moon clearly even with your binoculars. Try again the next night or when the next Full Moon is in the sky.

7. Moon watching

People have always watched the Moon because it is beautiful. People from long ago were also fascinated by the way it changed from a Full Moon to a New Moon and back. And they believed the Moon had special powers.

Moon celebrations

Long ago, many people believed the Moon was a goddess who helped crops grow and brought women healthy babies.

In a special African feast of the New Moon, only women were allowed to celebrate. Just before the rainy season, they danced all night and prayed to the Moon to give them children and food for the coming year.

In tales from Hawaii, the Moon was called *Hina-hanaia-i-ka-malama*, which means "the woman who works in the Moon."

The Latin word for Moon is *luna*, so anything to do with the Moon is called lunar. For instance, the Moon's orbit around the Earth is known as the lunar orbit.

Chinese people all over the world celebrate the New Year on the day of the second New Moon after the shortest day of the year — that's sometime between January 20 and February 20. They believe that seven days before the New Year, the kitchen god goes to the heavens to report on the doings of the family. Chinese people offer him sticky molasses so he can't speak up and say anything bad about them!

During the festival of the Eighth Moon during harvest time, Chinese people hold a celebration that includes dancing as well as parades with lit lanterns in different shapes. The most common lantern is a Moon shape, since it means perfect joy.

There are also many stories about strange things that happen under a Full Moon. Many people still believe that more crimes and weird things happen then. And there are lots of scary tales about people turning into wolves under the light of a Full Moon.

Why does the Moon look blue sometimes?

The Moon can look blue when there is lots of dust or dirt in the air, such as after a volcano erupts or a forest burns. The dust and ash act like filters and allow only the blue light in moonlight to shine through.

Every few years there are two Full Moons in one month. The second Full Moon is also called a Blue Moon, although no one knows why. But if you hear the saying "once in a Blue Moon," you know people mean something that doesn't happen often.

Can the Moon help you predict the weather?

When some people want to know the next day's weather, they don't turn on the radio, they look to the Moon. Many people believe that:

• A Full Moon on Saturday means rain on Sunday.

• Thunderstorms will happen two days after you see a New Moon.

• A pale Moon means rain is coming.

• A halo around the Moon means rain or snow.

Scientists don't believe most of these sayings but they agree a halo around the Moon often means rain or snow. The only time you see a halo is when there are lots of ice crystals high in the air. Lots of ice crystals mean clouds that will soon drop rain or, if it's cold, snow.

Try It!

Predict the weather with the Moon

You will need about five minutes each night for a month to do this project.

YOU WILL NEED

- a pencil
- a notebook

1 Watch the weather each day for a month. Report in your notebook if it was sunny or if it rained or snowed. Each night, look at the Moon and make a drawing of what you see. Write down the phase of the Moon (see page 52), whether the Moon is bright or pale and whether there is a ring.

2 When the month is over, look at your notes. Do you notice any patterns? If you saw a ring around the Moon, was there rain or snow the next day or the day after? Do any of the other sayings you just read about seem right?

You probably found that sometimes the sayings were right and sometimes they were wrong. Many things affect the weather, and the Moon can't tell you about all of them. Take another look at your notes, then make up your own sayings about the Moon and the weather.

What are tides?

Tides are the rise and fall of water in large lakes, oceans and seas. At low tide, the water is pulled away from the beach, so there's lots of room for you to build sand castles. But during high tide, the beach is covered with water.

Every day, on every ocean beach around the world, there are high tides and low tides. And they are caused by the Moon.

How does the Moon make tides?

As the Moon travels around Earth, the Moon's gravity pulls on the land and water on Earth. This pull changes the Earth's shape very slightly so that it bulges in two places. One bulge faces the Moon, the other bulge is on the opposite side of the Earth. Because water can flow easily over the Earth's surface, it gathers in these places and bulges even more than the land does. As the Earth spins, the two bulges move to stay in line with the Moon, producing two high tides and two low tides every day.

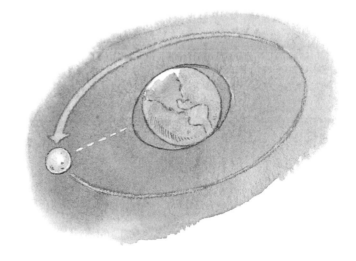

Try It!

Follow the tides

If you don't live near an ocean, you'll have to wait until you're on a visit there to try this experiment.

YOU WILL NEED

- an ocean beach
- a pencil
- a notebook

1 Look in the newspaper for the times when the high and low tides will happen. Draw what you see at high tide. Can you tell by watching the water when high tide starts to come in or go out?

2 Draw what you see at low tide. What does the beach look like now?

There are two high tides and two low tides every 24 hours and 50 minutes. You can find the exact time by checking in a newspaper. The time between high tide and low tide is always the same.

8. On the Moon

Ancient people only dreamed about traveling to the Moon. But by 1959, scientists in the United States and in the former Soviet Union had already built the first space rockets. The race was on to see which country could be the first to land astronauts on the Moon.

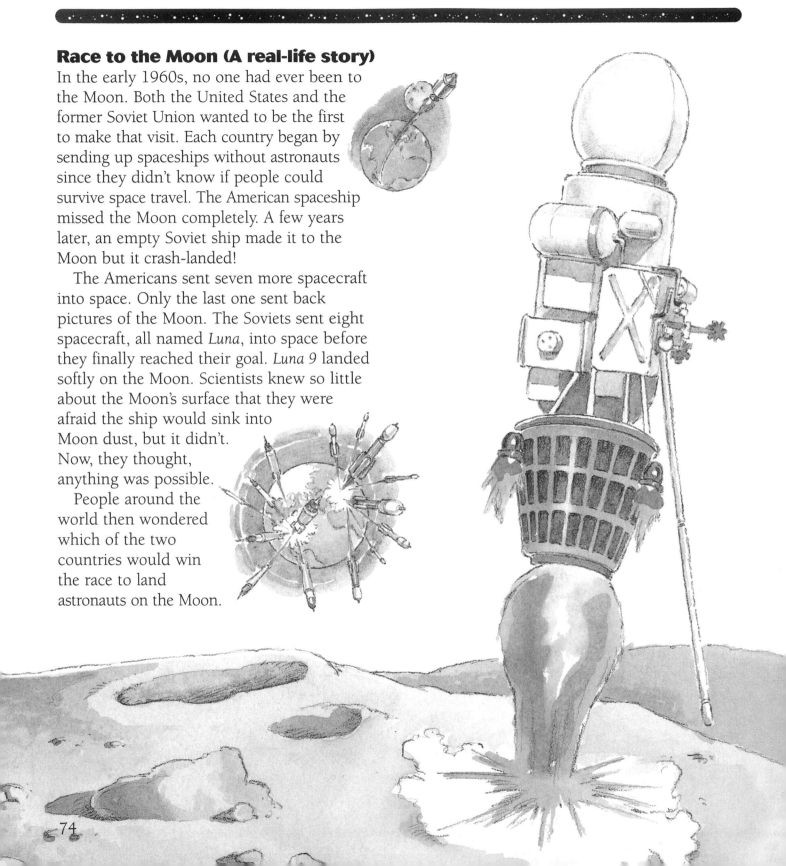

Race to the Moon (A real-life story)

In the early 1960s, no one had ever been to the Moon. Both the United States and the former Soviet Union wanted to be the first to make that visit. Each country began by sending up spaceships without astronauts since they didn't know if people could survive space travel. The American spaceship missed the Moon completely. A few years later, an empty Soviet ship made it to the Moon but it crash-landed!

The Americans sent seven more spacecraft into space. Only the last one sent back pictures of the Moon. The Soviets sent eight spacecraft, all named *Luna*, into space before they finally reached their goal. *Luna 9* landed softly on the Moon. Scientists knew so little about the Moon's surface that they were afraid the ship would sink into Moon dust, but it didn't. Now, they thought, anything was possible.

People around the world then wondered which of the two countries would win the race to land astronauts on the Moon.

Who was the first person on the Moon?

An American named Neil Armstrong was the first person to step on the Moon. The American spacecraft, *Apollo 11*, took 66 hours to make the trip from Earth. The main spacecraft orbited the Moon while two astronauts flew down to the surface in a small landing craft. On Sunday, July 20, 1969, Neil Armstrong and Edwin "Buzz" Aldrin landed on the Sea of Tranquility.

Neil Armstrong stepped out of the space capsule carrying a television camera. Everyone watching TV on Earth saw his first footstep onto the Moon. He said, "That's one small step for man, one giant leap for mankind."

Astronaut Neil Armstrong took this picture of "Buzz" Aldrin. You can also see the landing craft they used to land on the Moon's surface.

What did astronauts do on the Moon?

Astronauts collected samples of Moon dust and rock to bring back to Earth so scientists here could study them to learn more about the way the Moon was formed. The astronauts brought back 382 kg (842 lbs.) of Moon rock! They also explored the Moon's surface in "Moon buggies."

As well, the astronauts set up a device called a prism reflector. Scientists on Earth shine a laser beam at the Moon and this device reflects it back. The scientists know how quickly the light in the laser beam travels, so by measuring how long it takes for the light to return to Earth, they can tell more accurately than ever before how far the Moon is from Earth.

An astronaut scooping up Moon soil.

What's it like on the Moon?

The sky is black and there are no colorful sunsets because you need an atmosphere to scatter the light to see the colors in it.

There is no noise because sound needs air to travel.

Earth looks like a giant blue ball.

The Moon's gravity is only one-sixth as much as Earth's. If you weigh 36 kg (80 lbs.) on Earth, you'd weigh as little as a small dog on the Moon.

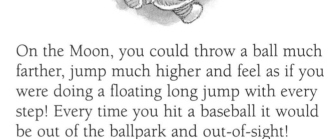

On the Moon, you could throw a ball much farther, jump much higher and feel as if you were doing a floating long jump with every step! Every time you hit a baseball it would be out of the ballpark and out-of-sight!

You would be taller on the Moon. On Earth, gravity pushes the bones in your back tightly together. But on the Moon, the lower gravity means your back bones aren't packed so tightly. The extra space gives you extra height.

Try It!

Measure your Moon strength

YOU WILL NEED

- 6 books*
- 6 cans of food*
- 6 shoes*
- a large cardboard box

* Use items that are about the same size as the other items in the same category.

1 Place all the items in the box.

2 Lift the box by crouching down and then straightening your legs. (This will protect your back.) Notice how heavy the box feels.

3 Take out five of each item. Leave only one book, one can and one shoe in the box.

4 Pretend you are on the Moon and the box still holds all the items. Lift the box again. How much lighter does it feel?

Because the Moon's mass is six times less than that of Earth, its pulling force — gravity — is only one-sixth as strong. That means things on the Moon weigh just one-sixth of their Earth weight. In other words, lifting a large object would be six times easier on the Moon.

Space Challenge: How much would you weigh on the Moon? (Answer on page 202.)

Will people ever live on the Moon?

Someday there will probably be a space station on the Moon. Many scientists would find it helpful. For example, astronomers could observe the universe from a Moon base. Since there is no atmosphere to cloud their view, they could see much more clearly from the Moon than from Earth.

The Moon station might also become a mining center for Earth. We are using up the metals and minerals here. But Moon rock is full of many of the minerals that we need and use.

Scientists might also make new medicines on the Moon. A germ-free place is needed for making drugs, and since there is no life on the Moon, there are no germs there.

Of course, for people to live on the Moon they will need food to eat, air to breathe, water to drink and gravity to help them move around comfortably. Right now we don't know how to do all these things, but in the future they may be possible. Perhaps you'll be the scientist who builds the first Moon base!

9. Our own star: The Sun

Ancient people knew the Sun brought light and warmth. But they didn't know what made it shine and where it went each night. So they made up stories to help them understand the secrets of the Sun.

Sun stories

Long ago, the Egyptians thought the sky goddess, Nut, swallowed the Sun every night and gave birth to a new Sun the next morning.

People in Lithuania in eastern Europe told a different story. The Sun and Moon fell in love and got married. They had a baby and named her Earth. But the parents were always fighting. The Moon told the Sun to stop being so hot. The Sun told the Moon to stop being cold. They decided to separate.

But they both wanted to keep Earth. When they couldn't decide what to do, they visited the great god Thunder. Thunder told the Sun to take care of her daughter from morning until evening and told the Moon to take care of Earth during the night. And that's the way it's always been. Once in a while, when the Moon is too busy, his sisters, the stars, shine on Earth.

If you see a word you don't know, look it up in the glossary on page 203.

80

What is the Sun?

The Sun is a star — a bright, big ball of superhot gas. It seems much larger than any other star because it is so much closer. The Sun is 150 million km (93 million mi.) away from Earth. That seems like a long way, but if the Sun were closer, nothing on Earth could survive the heat.

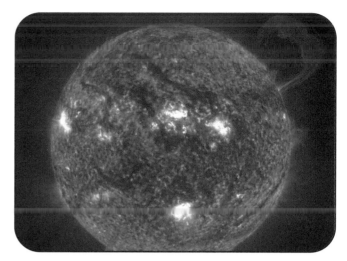

The big loop is a gigantic prominence (page 87).

SUN FACTS

- The Sun measures 1 392 000 km (865 000 mi.) across. If the Sun were an empty ball you could fit one million Earths inside it.

- The Sun weighs 2 billion billion billion t (tn). That's 2 with 27 zeros after it. That's 333 000 times as much as Earth!

- The Sun's gravity is 28 times greater than Earth's. If you weigh 45 kg (100 lbs.) on Earth, you'd weigh almost 1.5 t (tn) on the Sun!

- The Sun is 4.5 billion years old.

How big a star is the Sun?

Scientists have discovered that stars can range from dwarf to giant size. They can be even smaller than Earth or 100 times larger than the Sun. Stars can glow blue (which means they are very hot), white, yellow or red (much cooler). Our Sun is a medium-sized yellow star.

What does the Sun do?

The Sun gives us light and heat. The Sun's light makes plants grow. Plants give us food to eat and oxygen to breathe. We would die without them.

The Sun's heat gives us rain. When the Sun warms lakes and oceans, some of the water changes into a gas called water vapor. This gas floats high in the sky to where the air is cooler. The water vapor is chilled and changes back into water drops. When a lot of these drops join together, they form clouds. If the water drops get large enough, they fall as rain.

The Sun's heat also gives us wind. The heat warms the air, and when air is warm, it moves. And wind is moving air.

If there were no Sun, Earth would have no wind, rain, heat or light.

When did the Sun start to shine?

The Sun started to shine 4.5 billion years ago. Long, long before that, there were nothing but gases floating around in the universe. About 12 billion years ago, pockets of gas gathered together to form the Milky Way galaxy. Over time, hundreds of billions of stars were born inside the Milky Way

Our Sun was one of those stars. It started as an enormous cool cloud of gas and dust. It became smaller and hotter until it started to shine.

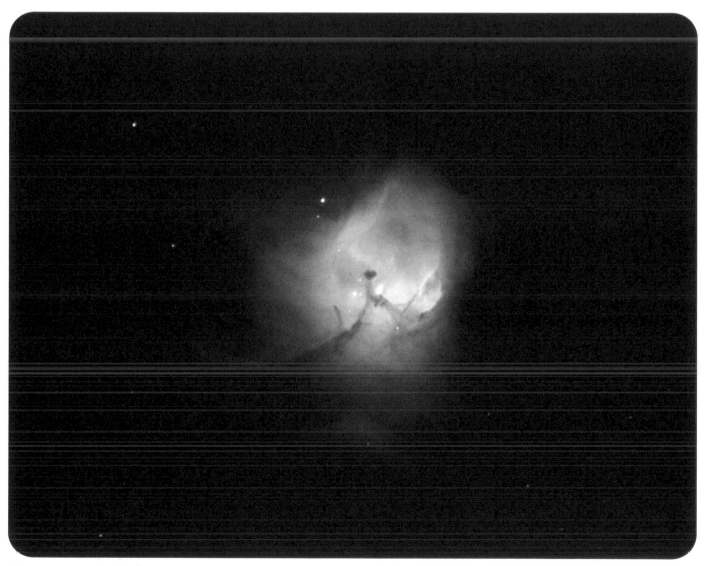

The Sun was born in a huge cloud of gas and dust like the one shown in this space photo.

Why does the Sun shine?

It all starts in the Sun's center, also known as its core. The Sun's core is hotter than any furnace on Earth. All the weight of the huge, heavy Sun presses on its core. As the hydrogen gas near the core becomes superhot and super squished, it turns into helium gas and gives off huge blasts of energy as it changes.

Every second, 4 million t (4.4 million tn) of hydrogen change into helium and energy. But don't worry about the Sun using up all its hydrogen. There is enough hydrogen in the Sun to keep it shining for another 6 billion years.

The energy the Sun makes as the hydrogen changes to helium starts moving from the Sun's core toward the outside. But because the Sun is so large and heavy, it takes millions of years for the energy to pass through it. When the energy finally reaches the Sun's surface, some of it turns into waves of light and heat that move outward very quickly through the emptiness of space. On Earth you can see the Sun's light waves, or sunshine, and you can feel the heat!

Will the Sun shine forever?

No, all stars die. In about 6 billion years the Sun will start to glow red and grow bigger. It will become so hot that the ice at Earth's North Pole will melt and the oceans will begin to boil. The Sun will continue to grow until it swallows the planets closest to it — including Earth! Then the Sun will begin to shrink and become dimmer and dimmer until it is a small, dim star called a white dwarf.

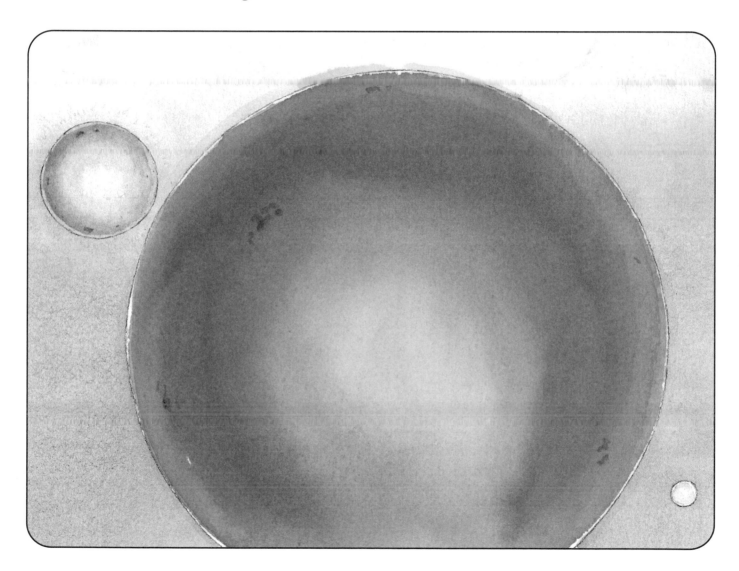

What have space probes revealed about the Sun?

The American probe *Ulysses* passed over the Sun's south pole in 1994 and its north pole in 1995. *Ulysses* discovered that the Sun is surrounded by a huge magnetic field and that its solar winds can reach incredible speeds of up to 3.2 million km/h (2 million m.p.h.).

What does the Sun look like?

You should never look at the Sun, not even with strong sunglasses. Your eyes focus the Sun's light onto a small spot inside them. That makes the light strong enough to burn your eyes and make you blind. However, scientists have machines that let them look at the Sun so they can see its different parts.

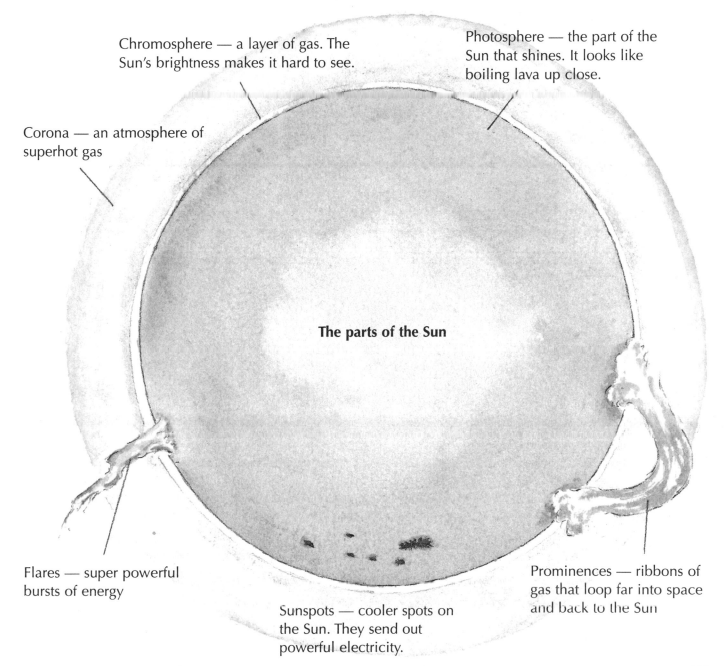

Chromosphere — a layer of gas. The Sun's brightness makes it hard to see.

Photosphere — the part of the Sun that shines. It looks like boiling lava up close.

Corona — an atmosphere of superhot gas

The parts of the Sun

Flares — super powerful bursts of energy

Sunspots — cooler spots on the Sun. They send out powerful electricity.

Prominences — ribbons of gas that loop far into space and back to the Sun

Try It!

Look at the Sun safely

YOU WILL NEED

- a sunny day
- tape
- a large piece of white paper
- a small square of cardboard
- a small nail
- a stake or stick
- a bucket of sand
- a mirror

1 Tape the paper to a wall outside.

2 Have an adult punch a hole in the center of the cardboard with the nail. Tape the cardboard to the stick — don't put the hole in front of the stick!

3 Stand the stick in the bucket of sand. Place the bucket in front of the paper on the wall.

4 Ask a friend to hold the mirror and move it until it reflects the Sun through the hole in the cardboard. Look at the white paper until you see an image of the Sun. Draw what you see.

Looking at the Sun this way is a safe way to get an idea of how the Sun looks. Did you see any dark spots on the Sun? These are sunspots. Repeat this project a few days later and compare your pictures. You'll see that not all the sunspots are in the same place in both pictures. That's because sunspots move as the Sun spins.

What is a solar eclipse?

Imagine you're outside on a clear, sunny day. Suddenly the sky begins to turn dark. There's a dark hole on one side of the Sun and the hole is getting bigger! Soon all that is left of the Sun is a halo of sparkling light around a black circle. On Earth the sky is as dark as night. The birds are silent and the air feels colder. There is an eerie quiet.

Is the Sun dying? No — an eclipse is taking place. Sometimes the Sun, Moon and Earth line up in a straight line with the Moon in the middle. The Moon blocks the Sun's light from reaching Earth and a solar eclipse occurs.

If the Moon blocks all the Sun's light, it causes a total eclipse of the Sun. When only part of the Sun's light is blocked, a partial eclipse of the Sun takes place. As the Earth and Moon continue in their orbits and move out of line, more and more sunlight appears. The eclipse is over.

When is the next eclipse?

There are usually two to four solar eclipses each year. You'll experience a total eclipse only if where you live is completely in the Moon's shadow.

DATE	Where total eclipse will be seen
August 1, 2008	Canada, northern Europe, Asia
July 22, 2009	Asia, Pacific, Hawaii
July 11, 2010	South Pacific, South America
November 13, 2012	Australia, New Zealand, South America

What is a sundial?

A sundial is a clock that uses the Sun to tell time. The pointer on the sundial casts a shadow onto a disk that has lines marked on it. These markings each have a time of day written beside them. As the Earth turns throughout the day, the pointer's shadow moves across the disk. If the shadow falls on the line marked 11, then it is 11:00 in the morning.

The early Egyptians were among the first people to discover how to use the Sun to tell time. Their sundials, or shadow clocks, were made of just a stick stuck in the ground, with lines scratched in the earth around it.

The stick is called a *gnomon* (say it NO-mun) from the Greek word meaning "one who knows."

Try It!

Make your own sundial

Start this project early in the morning. You'll need to spend a few minutes with it every hour throughout the day.

YOU WILL NEED

- a sunny day
- an open sunny place
- a small ball of modeling clay
- a piece of cardboard about 25 cm x 25 cm (10 in. x 10 in.)
- a small stick
- a watch
- a pencil

1 Place the modeling clay in the middle of one of the edges of the cardboard.

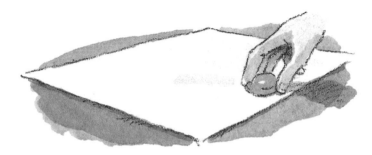

2 Stand the stick straight up in the middle of modeling clay as shown.

3 Put your sundial in a sunny place so that the stick's shadow falls on the cardboard.

4 Mark the spot where the shadow falls on your cardboard. Write down the time beside it. Your sundial will be easier to use if you mark the shadow's position on the hour. Do this every hour until the Sun goes down.

If you leave your sundial where it is, you can use it to tell time on any sunny day. If the stick's shadow is between your marks, you can tell the time by deciding which of the marks the shadow is closer to. You'll probably quickly discover why people now use clocks instead of sundials. Sundials can't tell time at night or on cloudy days.

10. The Sun's light

What color is sunlight? You may think it's yellow, but in this chapter you'll find out that's only part of the answer. You'll also discover how the Sun's light makes rainbows and why sunsets are so incredibly beautiful.

How the sky got a rainbow

When you look at a rainbow, does it remind you of a snake? The Shoshone people of the northwestern United States thought so. They told this story to explain the appearance of the first rainbow.

Long ago, in a time when there was no rain and the people had no food or water, a magical snake told the Shoshone to throw him into the air. What could a snake do? the people wondered. The snake begged them again to throw him into the air. Finally, a shaman, a man with magical powers, threw the snake upward. The snake stretched until he reached across the sky.

Then he arched his back and changed from one color to another.

The snake rubbed his scales against the sky until rain fell from the clouds. When the rains were done, the people danced with joy and the Sun started to shine again. Now whenever the Sun shines after a rain, the snake comes out to show his colors.

What color is sunlight?

The sunlight you see every day looks white but it is really a mixture of seven different colors: red, orange, yellow, green, blue, indigo and violet. The colors are always the same and they are always arranged in the same order.

How can you see all the colors in sunlight?

You can only see all the colors when sunlight is split up. One way this happens is when sunlight shines through glass cut into a special shape called a prism.

Light slows down when it goes through a prism and changes direction. Another way to say this is that light bends or refracts. Violet — the color that travels the slowest — makes the sharpest change in direction. Red travels the fastest and makes a small change in direction.

Try It!

Make a rainbow

YOU WILL NEED

- a sunny day
- a prism, crystal glass or a piece of cut crystal such as a glass animal (ask permission)
- a piece of white paper

1 Put the prism or other crystal where the sun will shine on it.

2 Hold the paper as shown so that the light coming through the prism hits the paper. What do you see on the paper?

What you see is a rainbow — all the colors in light. How are rainbows formed in the sky? After it rains there are raindrops still in the air. Each raindrop acts as a prism splitting the light into all its colors. If you're standing with the Sun behind you and air with lots of water drops in it (such as just after it rains) in front of you, you will see a rainbow.

Why is the sky blue and a sunset red?

When the Sun is high in the sky during the day, some of the blue light in the sunlight is scattered by Earth's atmosphere and the sky looks blue. When the Sun is low in the sky at sunset, more of the other colors are scattered too, and the sky becomes more colorful.

After a volcano erupts, you'll see redder sunsets because fine dust and ash in the air can scatter the red light.

The setting Sun looks red because Earth's atmosphere bends the other colors of sunlight away from our eyes.

Try It!

Find out why sunsets are red

YOU WILL NEED

- a dark room
- a table
- a clear bowl
- water
- an eyedropper or spoon
- low-fat milk
- a piece of white paper
- a flashlight

1 Fill the bowl with water. Add a few drops of milk until the water seems cloudy.

2 Hold the white paper as shown behind the bowl.

3 Hold the flashlight so that the light shines through the milky water and reflects on the white paper. What colors do you see on the paper?

You should see a reddish color like the color of a sunset. The milk in the water scatters the light just as the gases in the atmosphere scatter light.

What is UV light?

UV, or ultraviolet, light is invisible light from the Sun. Most UV light is absorbed by a gas in Earth's atmosphere called ozone. But some passes through. This UV light gives your skin a tan by making it produce a brown chemical called melanin. Too much UV light can give you a sunburn and harm plants and animals.

What is the ozone layer?

About 40 km (25 mi.) above Earth there is a thin layer of a gas called ozone. One of the most important things ozone does is stop too much UV light from reaching Earth.

Chemicals known as chlorofluorocarbons, or CFCs, eat up ozone. CFCs get into the atmosphere when refrigerators and air conditioners are destroyed. Around the world there are laws to cut down on the use of CFCs and keep the ozone layer safe.

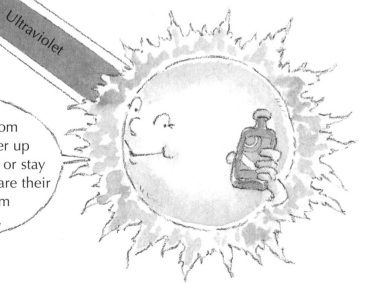

Ozone

Ultraviolet

To protect your skin from too much UV light, cover up in the Sun, use a sunblock or stay inside when the Sun's rays are their most powerful — from 10 a.m. until 4 p.m.

What are the northern lights?

The northern lights are the colorful, dancing bands of light that appear in the night sky over countries such as Canada that are close to the North Pole. They are also called the aurora borealis.

The auroras are caused by a weird wind called a solar wind. Every second, many tons of bits of the Sun are blown into space, forming a wind of small particles moving away from the Sun. Near the Earth, some of these particles are trapped by an invisible shield called the Earth's magnetic field.

The magnetic field pulls the particles toward the North and South Poles. As they are pulled lower, they collide with gases in Earth's atmosphere, causing them to glow and shimmer across the sky.

Near the South Pole, the colorful bands of lights are called the southern lights or aurora australis.

11. Using the Sun's energy

The Sun gives us more than light. We can use the Sun's energy for power and it also keeps us warm. Learn about the Sun's rays and how we use them every day.

This aircraft can be completely powered by the solar energy cells on its wings.

A story about the Sun's energy

The Algonkian people of Canada tell this legend that warns about the scorching heat of the Sun.

Tcakabesh lived with his sister in the forest where he hunted and fished for food.

One day he went to the place where the Sun meets the sky to lay a trap to catch some supper.

The next day the Sun did not rise.

"Go and see what has happened to the Sun," said his sister.

Tcakabesh hurried to the place where the Sun meets the sky. There, inside his trap, was the Sun! Tcakabesh tried to free it, but he couldn't get close because the Sun was too hot. He asked all the animals to help. "If we do not," he pleaded, "there will always be darkness."

The animals tried, one after the other, to free the Sun. The squirrel tried to bite the ropes, but the Sun was too hot. It made the squirrel's tail turn up at the end and it is still that way.

Finally, the mouse tried. He nibbled right through the ropes. The hair on his back was singed off and it is still that way. But the mouse freed the Sun. The Sun rose into the sky and was never trapped again.

101

What are heat rays?

Heat rays are just one of the many kinds of rays that come from the Sun. You can feel them when you stand in sunlight. They make your skin feel warm.

We only feel a tiny part of all the heat rays the Sun sends out. That's a good thing — if all the Sun's heat rays hit Earth, everything would burn up!

Why do some things get hotter in the Sun than others?

Everything heats up at different speeds. Air heats up faster than water — that's why you can take a cool dip in a pool on a hot day. Light colors reflect heat, so they stay cooler, and dark colors absorb heat, so they stay warmer. Shiny, smooth surfaces also reflect heat, while rough, dull surfaces keep heat in.

Try It!

Find the warmest color

YOU WILL NEED

- a sunny day
- 5 ice cubes
- squares of colored paper in black, white, red, blue and yellow
- a clock or watch

1 Put an ice cube in the center of each piece of paper.

2 Time how long it takes each ice cube to melt. Which one melts the fastest?

The faster an ice cube melts, the more heat the paper it is on absorbs. Which color absorbs heat the fastest? Which absorbs heat the slowest?

You might notice the same effect with your clothing. A jacket or shirt made from a dark fabric absorbs more heat and will keep you warmer.

103

What is solar power?

Solar power is power we get from the Sun. We use the Sun's energy to warm buildings, heat water and make electricity.

One way we gather the Sun's energy is in solar panels — black boxes with glass tops. (You already found out on page 103 how well black absorbs light.) You can see these boxes on the roofs of buildings. Water flowing through the solar panels is warmed by the Sun. That warm water then runs through pipes in the building to keep the rooms warm.

Solar cells are another way we use the Sun's power. They turn the Sun's light into electricity to power watches, calculators and even space satellites. Solar power will become even more important in the future as we use up fuels such as wood, coal and oil.

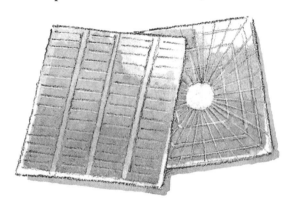

How do plants use the Sun?

Plants use sunlight to make food. When the Sun shines on green plants, it starts a process in their leaves that creates food. While plants make food, they take in carbon dioxide gas and breathe out oxygen. You breathe in oxygen and breathe out carbon dioxide. So plants and people depend on each other and we all depend on the Sun.

You can tell plants need the Sun — watch how they turn toward it!

Why study the Sun?

People have always been fascinated by the Sun. The Mayan Indians, who lived long ago in Mexico and Central America, built huge observatories so they could follow the Sun and find out more about the glowing ball they depended on.

Scientists today study the Sun so they can discover more about how it shines with such a steady light. In 1976, a solar probe called *Helios 2* came closer to the Sun than any spacecraft ever had. It came within 45 million km (28 million mi.) of the Sun — any closer and it would have fried in the Sun's heat!

As more and more people are born on our planet, we use up more and more of our power resources, such as gas, coal and oil. But the Sun is an unlimited resource. Studying the Sun helps us learn how we can use its power. Perhaps one day we will be able to harness the energy of the Sun to power everything on Earth.

As the Sun sets, the space shuttle *Discovery* rolls out to its launchpad at the Kennedy Space Center.

12. The solar system: Planets

Imagine living without computers, DVDs and electric lights. What would you do on dark nights? People long ago watched the stars. They noticed a few strange dots of light that moved through the stars. They called these moving lights planets, a word that means wanderers.

This artist's view of the solar system shows all the planets plus the four large moons of Jupiter as though they were gathered together in one part of the sky.

Planet stories

Long ago, people thought the sky was full of magic. They believed that the motions of the planets changed what happened here on Earth.

Early Tahitians worried when Venus and Jupiter were close together in the sky. "The planets are threatening each other," they said. "That means two of our chiefs will soon go to war."

An ancient Chinese poem says the planet Mars landed on Earth in the shape of a young boy. He told the people all about the future, then flew back up into the sky.

The Pawnee people of North America watched the planets cross the wide open skies and said, "If people die of sickness, the planets will take care of their souls."

If you see a word you don't know, look it up in the glossary on page 203.

What is a planet?

A planet is a large round object that travels around the Sun. Its path is clear of other objects. Earth is a planet. Mercury, Venus, Mars, Jupiter, Saturn, Uranus and Neptune are also planets. Pluto used to be called a planet. It is round and circles the Sun, but its path is not clear of other objects. In 2006, astronomers decided to change Pluto's title to "dwarf planet."

The Sun and the objects of our solar system

Sun

Mercury

Venus

Earth

Mars

Jupiter

Saturn

Uranus

Neptune

Pluto

What is the solar system?

The solar system is made up of the Sun and the objects circling it. In the solar system, there are 8 planets and more than 100 moons. Thousands of small, rocky lumps called asteroids also circle the Sun. Most of them are between Mars and Jupiter. Far beyond the orbits of the planets is a swarm of icy comets. Their orbits sometimes take them close to the Sun, where they are visible from Earth.

How do planets move?

The planets travel around the Sun in almost circular paths called orbits. The Sun's pulling force — gravity — keeps them from flying off into space.

Each planet also rotates around an imaginary axis. Most planets spin with their axes pointing nearly up and down. But Uranus spins on its side.

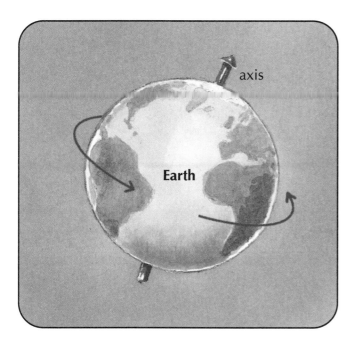

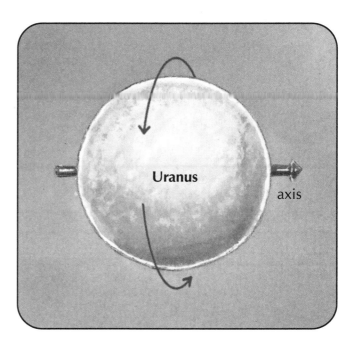

Why do planets shine?

Planets shine when the Sun's light bounces off them. Unlike stars, they don't glow with their own heat.

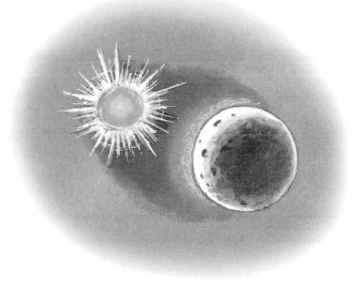

How did the solar system begin?

Scientists believe that the solar system took shape from an enormous swirling cloud of gas and dust particles. In the center of the cloud, particles clumped together and formed a new star, the Sun. Other particles continued to flow like a whirlpool around the Sun. About 4.5 billion years ago, the cloud separated into many smaller lumps. They became the planets, moons, asteroids and comets of the solar system.

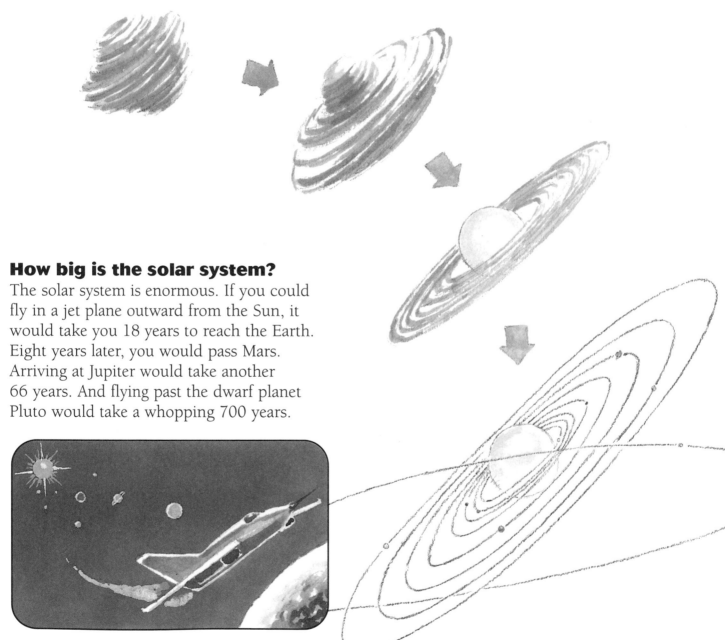

How big is the solar system?

The solar system is enormous. If you could fly in a jet plane outward from the Sun, it would take you 18 years to reach the Earth. Eight years later, you would pass Mars. Arriving at Jupiter would take another 66 years. And flying past the dwarf planet Pluto would take a whopping 700 years.

Try It!

Make a solar system you can eat

If the planets were the sizes of the foods shown here, the Sun would be as big as a passenger van. And the distances between planets would be enormous. For example, Neptune would be 6 km (3.7 mi.) away from Mercury.

1 Can you put the foods in the order of planets in the solar system?

YOU WILL NEED

- a large honeydew or small watermelon
- a cantaloupe
- 2 large round apples
- 2 cherries
- a small raspberry
- a pea

Neptune

Uranus

Mars

Saturn

Earth

Mercury

Venus

Jupiter

111

Exploring the solar system

How do you explore a place that's too dangerous or distant for humans? Send in the robots! In the past 40 years, robotic spacecraft have transformed our ideas about far-off planets — and other parts of our vast solar system.

Mariner 10 took more than 3000 photos of Venus in 1974.

What is a space probe?

A space probe is a robotic spacecraft with no people on board. It can travel much further, and stay in space much longer, than a spacecraft with a human crew. A space probe is powered by nuclear or solar energy and is remotely controlled from Earth by radio signals.

Probes gather data by taking photographs and using radar to measure landforms. Some gather soil and air samples. Others perform experiments to detect signs of life. Without space probes, we would know much less about our neighbors in the solar system.

How does a space probe send data to Earth?

A space probe uses radio signals to beam information to Earth. These signals are in the digital form computers use. Some signals produce images that show a distant planet's surface. Others carry information about the planet's temperature and atmosphere.

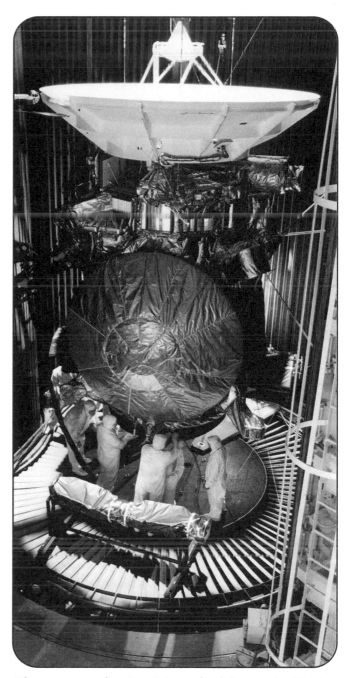

The space probe *Cassini* reached Saturn in 2004. It has revealed many new details of the planet's moons and rings.

Mercury: Racing around the Sun

If you've ever stood near a hot fire on a cold night, you have some idea how Mercury feels. The side facing the Sun sizzles while the side facing away freezes.

Mercury has tall mountains, steep cliffs and broad, flat plains. The plains probably formed long ago, when lava from inside the planet flooded its surface.

What would it be like to visit Mercury?

As you zoom in on Mercury, you might think you are landing on the Moon. Like the Moon, Mercury is spotted with craters formed when asteroids and meteoroids crashed into it.

Mercury has hardly any air, so you'd need oxygen tanks to breathe. You'd also need a special suit to protect you from the extreme cold and heat. Even with all the heavy gear, you'd be able to leap farther and jump higher than on Earth. Mercury's low gravity means you weigh about one-third of your Earth weight.

Why is Mercury so hot – and cold?

Mercury is close to the Sun, so it gets more intense heat than Earth does. On the side facing the sun it is HOT. But it has no blanket of air to keep heat in.
So on the side facing away from the sun, it is COLD.

Mercury's temperature changes are the greatest of any planet.

What's inside Mercury?

Inside its rocky outer crust, Mercury has a large core of iron. Because Mercury's core is so big for its size, some scientists think Mercury may once have been much bigger. How did it shrink? A collision with a giant asteroid may have knocked off much of its outer layer.

MERCURY FACTS

- Mercury rotates on its axis once every 58 days and 14 hours.

- Mercury orbits the Sun in just 88 days, compared with Earth's 365.2 days. Because of the planet's speed, early Roman sky watchers named it after Mercury, the messenger god who sped through the sky on winged feet.

- Mercury is the closest planet to the Sun.

- Mercury is only a little bigger than our moon.

- Craters on Mercury are named after famous composers, authors and artists such as Beethoven, Vivaldi, Dickens and Renoir.

Venus: Sky dazzler

Have you ever wished upon a star? Chances are it wasn't a star at all. Often, the first bright light in the evening sky is Venus, the closest planet to Earth.

The atmosphere of Venus traps the Sun's heat, making it the hottest planet in the solar system.

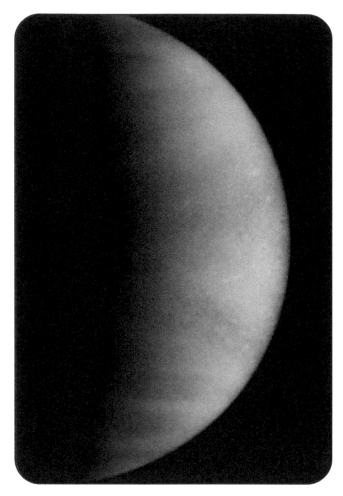

This picture of Venus was taken by the Hubble Space Telescope. The thick clouds that blanket Venus make it difficult to photograph the surface.

What would it be like to visit Venus?

Watch out for lightning as you descend through the yellow clouds of Venus. But don't worry about rain — water evaporates instantly in the heat. On Venus's dry, rocky surface, the temperature reaches 460°C (860°F). That's hot enough to melt lead — and your spaceship.

Need more reasons to avoid Venus? Its atmosphere is poisonous. And the planet's air pressure would crush you instantly. It's 90 times stronger than air pressure on Earth.

116

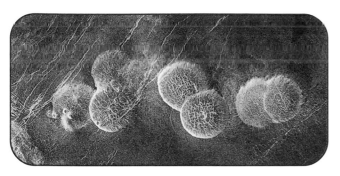

These domes on Venus formed when lava spurted out of volcanoes. Scientists aren't sure if Venus's volcanoes are still active.

Why does Venus look so bright?

Venus is completely covered in a thick blanket of yellowish clouds. These clouds reflect sunlight, making the planet shine in the evening or early morning sky.

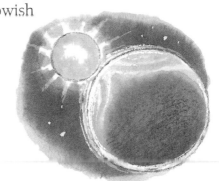

VENUS FACTS

- A year on Venus is 224.7 days long. That's how long it takes Venus to orbit the Sun.

- Venus rotates on its axis once every 243 days and 5 hours.

- Venus has no moons.

- Venus is sometimes called Earth's twin because it is almost the same size as Earth.

- Venus looks so beautiful that people wanted to give it a beautiful name. They called it Venus, after the Roman goddess of love.

- Earth rotates from west to east. Venus rotates in the opposite direction.

- Almost all the landforms on Venus are named after women, such as the Greek goddess Aphrodite and the pilot Amelia Earhart.

Mars: A red mystery

Is there life on Mars? People have asked that question for centuries. They've imagined bug-eyed Martians with dangling tentacles. But recent clues point to a strange new story of Martian life.

Mars looks reddish because of rust in its iron-rich soil. This color reminded people of anger and blood, so they named the planet after the Roman god of war.

Mars is a cold place. Its polar ice caps are made of ice and frozen carbon dioxide, sometimes called dry ice.

What would it be like to visit Mars?

Admire the peach-colored sky as you descend toward Mars. But don't be tempted to step out onto the rust-colored soil. The atmosphere is so thin you'd be instantly sunburned by the Sun's harmful rays. The low air pressure would make your blood bubble. And Martian air is almost all carbon dioxide, the stuff you breathe out.

This picture from the 1997 Pathfinder mission shows the *Sojourner* rover on the rocky surface of Mars. The large rock was named Yogi.

Clues from Mars: A true story

When Roberta Score picked up a rock in Antarctica in 1984, she didn't know she was holding a piece of Mars.

The greenish, potato-size rock was sent to NASA's Johnson Space Center in Texas. It was stored there for ten years. Then scientists began to check it out.

Inside the rock they found air bubbles that matched Martian air samples. They also discovered minerals that are sometimes produced by living things.

Powerful microscopes revealed tiny tubelike structures, each far thinner than a human hair. Were these fossils of ancient creatures?

In 1996, NASA scientists announced that the rock was formed on Mars about 4.5 billion years ago. It was thrown into space when an asteroid or comet crashed into the planet. After circling the Sun for 15 million years, the Martian meteorite landed on Earth.

The meteorite may show that life once existed on Mars. But scientists want more proof. New space probes will collect more samples. And scientists will continue to test Roberta Score's rock.

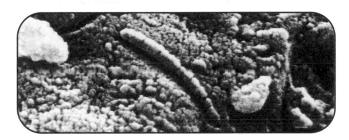

MARS FACTS

- A Martian year is 687 Earth days long. That's how long it takes Mars to orbit the Sun.

- Mars rotates on its axis once every 24 hours and 37 minutes, so a Martian day is almost the same length as an Earth day.

- Because Mars is tilted like the Earth, it has seasons.

- Mars has two small, potato-shaped moons named Phobos and Deimos. These Greek words mean "fear" and "panic."

- Mars is about half the size of Earth.

- Olympus Mons on Mars is the highest known mountain in the solar system. This volcano is three times taller than Mount Everest.

Try It!

Test for signs of life

YOU WILL NEED

- 3 tall drinking glasses labeled 1, 2 and 3
- 250 mL (1 c.) cornmeal
- 15 mL (1 tbsp.) baking soda
- 15 mL (1 tbsp.) yeast
- 125 mL (1/2 c.) sugar
- 500 mL (2 c.) warm water
- a spoon

1 Divide the cornmeal among the three glasses. Add the baking soda to glass 2. Add the yeast to glass 3.

2 Dissolve the sugar in the warm water.

3 Pour one-third of the sugar and water solution into each glass. Stir gently. Check the glasses after 1 minute, 10 minutes and again after 20 minutes. What do you see?

No reaction means no life. A quick fizzing shows an ordinary chemical reaction — still no life. But a reaction that starts slowly and lasts a long time means you've found something alive and growing.

In 1976, a space probe did similar tests on soil samples from Mars. Scientists were looking for a long, slow reaction. The space probe tests showed no signs of life. What did your test find? Answer on page 202.

Jupiter: A gas giant

If you wanted to land a spaceship on Jupiter, you'd have a major problem. Why? There's no land to land on!

The Great Red Spot is a hurricane that has raged on Jupiter for at least 300 years. It is so huge that three Earths could fit inside it.

What would it be like to visit Jupiter?

Jupiter doesn't have a solid surface like Earth. Instead, it's made of thick gases. Visiting Jupiter would be like trying to land on a cloud.

The pull of gravity at Jupiter's surface is 2.5 times stronger than on Earth, so you would quickly be pulled deeper into the planet.

Scientists think Jupiter might have a small, solid inner core wrapped in an ocean of liquid hydrogen and helium. But you'd be crushed and cooked by the immense pressure and heat of Jupiter's inner layers before you reached the core.

Discovering Jupiter's moons: A true story

In 1609, in northern Italy, a math professor by the name of Galileo Galilei heard news of a marvelous invention. By mounting two lenses inside a tube, you could see distant objects as if they were nearby.

Galileo quickly constructed a telescope for himself. On January 7, 1610, he aimed his new instrument at Jupiter and made an astounding discovery. Lined up beside the planet were three small bodies. Galileo called them "starlets." As he watched from night to night, the three bodies moved and a fourth one appeared. Galileo soon realized that he was watching four moons revolving around Jupiter.

At the time, most people believed Earth was the center of the universe. Now Galileo had proof that some things did *not* revolve around Earth. If moons circled Jupiter, he argued, was it not possible that all the planets, including Earth, revolve around the Sun?

Galileo's ideas so shocked people that he was locked in his house for the last nine years of his life. Even so, Galileo's ideas changed astronomy forever. Nearly 400 years later, a space probe began taking close-up photos of Jupiter and its many moons. The name of the probe? *Galileo*.

Jupiter with its moons Io, Europa, Ganymede and Callisto. Jupiter has over 60 moons.

Why does Jupiter look striped?

Jupiter's stripes are bands of pink, red, yellow, tan and white clouds. The lightest bands are called zones. They are made of ice crystals of ammonia. Darker bands, called belts, contain traces of other chemicals. Strong winds and Jupiter's rapid spin stretch the clouds into stripes.

Jupiter's multicolored clouds.

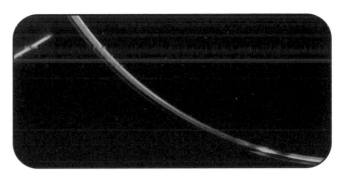

Jupiter, the largest planet, surprised scientists in 1979. Two *Voyager* probes revealed a thin ring circling this giant ball of gases. In 1994, when pieces of Comet Shoemaker-Levy 9 crashed into Jupiter, the *Galileo* space probe took photos and sent them back to Earth.

JUPITER FACTS

- A Jupiter year is about 11.9 Earth years long. That's how long it takes Jupiter to orbit the Sun.

- Jupiter rotates on its axis once every 9 hours and 50 minutes.

- If Jupiter were hollow, all the other planets would fit inside it.

- Because it was so big and bright in the sky, early Romans named Jupiter after their chief god.

Try It!

Make a model of Jupiter's stormy surface

YOU WILL NEED

- 150 mL (2/3 c.) milk
- a large pie plate
- red and yellow food coloring
- liquid dish detergent

1 Pour the milk into the pie plate.

2 Gently add two drops of red food coloring to one half of the milk.

3 Add two drops of yellow food coloring to the other half.

4 Carefully drop detergent into the center of each spot of food coloring.

5 Spin the plate gently two or three times to mix the colors. Watch the swirling bands and pretend you are in a spaceship approaching Jupiter.

Saturn: Rings of wonder

If you had to pick the most beautiful planet, which would it be? What about Saturn with its multicolored rings?

What would it be like to visit Saturn?

The view as you approach the planet would be spectacular. No other planet has such a broad and colorful system of rings.

You could hover a while in Saturn's cold upper clouds, but don't descend. Scientists believe Saturn might have a liquid interior and small, rocky core. But like Jupiter, Saturn is made mostly of hydrogen and helium gases that become hotter and denser toward its center. Get too close and you might be squished and roasted.

Why does Saturn have rings?

Saturn's rings may have formed when a small moon drifted too close to the planet and was ripped to pieces. Bits of dust and ice, from the size of a pea to the size of a house, spread around the planet in thousands of separate rings.

Saturn's ring system is about 1 km (0.6 mi.) thick.

Does Saturn have moons?

Saturn has over 30 named moons, plus many smaller moons that haven't yet been named. The major moons are outside Saturn's rings.

Titan, the largest moon, is bigger than the planet Mercury. It is the only moon known to have a dense atmosphere. Enceladus is covered with smooth ice, making it the shiniest body in the solar system. Iapetus is white on one side and black on the other.

Saturn with four of its moons.

SATURN FACTS

- A year on Saturn is 29.5 Earth years long. That's how long it takes Saturn to orbit the Sun.

- Saturn is not as dense as Earth. If you could find a swimming pool big enough, Saturn would float.

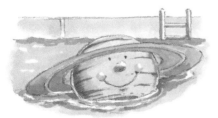

- Saturn rotates on its axis once every 10 hours and 14 minutes.

- Because Saturn moves slowly and steadily across the sky, early people said it was like an old man. Ancient Romans called the planet Saturn after the old father of Jupiter.

Try It!

See some planets for yourself

You don't need a telescope to see Venus, Jupiter, Mars, Mercury and Saturn. Here are some tips on how to find planets in the night sky. Happy hunting!

1 Call a planetarium or look in the latest issue of an astronomy magazine to find out which planets can be seen this month and where they can be found.

2 Without staring directly at the Sun, notice where it crosses the sky during the day. At night, you can find the planets near this same band of sky.

3 Find a viewing place away from bright lights, tall trees and buildings. Use a compass to find north, south, east and west. You'll need to know these directions to find your way around the sky.

Once you've found Jupiter, check it out with binoculars. You should be able to see some of its moons.

You can usually find Venus by looking east just before sunrise or west just after sunset. The planet looks like an extremely bright star low in the sky.

One way to tell if something is a planet is that planets don't twinkle like stars do. They shine steadily.

Uranus: Rolling along

The giant planet Uranus rolls along its path around the Sun on its side. Some scientists think something big may have crashed into Uranus and knocked it over.

Uranus's narrow rings are made of chunks of black ice.

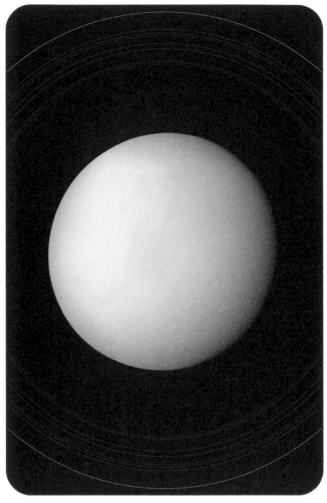

Uranus with its icy rings.

What would it be like to visit Uranus?

As you head toward Uranus, watch for its narrow, black rings. They're much harder to see than those of Saturn.

Methane gas in the upper atmosphere gives Uranus a blue-green color. As you descend, your spaceship is surrounded by a cold, unbreathable fog of hydrogen and helium. Fierce winds blow you along at 700 km/h (435 m.p.h.), making landing difficult. But that doesn't matter because there's nowhere to land. Like Jupiter and Saturn, Uranus is a gas planet.

Does Uranus have moons?

Uranus has over 25 moons. Ten of them were discovered by the *Voyager 2* spacecraft in 1986. Titania, the biggest, is about half the size of our moon. Scientists think an asteroid may have shattered the moon Miranda. When the pieces fell back together, the tiny moon looked like a patchwork quilt.

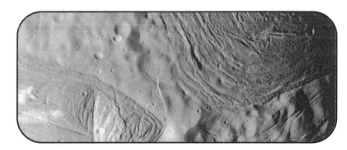

Uranus's moon Miranda with its patchwork surface.

URANUS FACTS

- A Uranus year is 84 Earth years long. That's how long it takes Uranus to orbit the Sun.

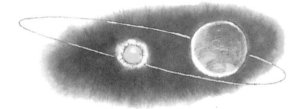

- Uranus rotates on its side once every 17 hours and 14 minutes.

- Uranus was the first planet to be discovered with a telescope. It was sighted in 1781.

- Scientists think that Uranus may have an inner liquid layer surrounding a rocky core.

- Some people wanted to name Uranus after its discoverer, a music teacher named William Herschel. But instead it was named after Uranus, father of Saturn and grandfather of Jupiter in Roman myths.

Neptune: Another blue planet

Neptune looks like a tropical sea, blue and beautiful. But don't bother getting out the beach towels — this planet is anything but tropical.

Methane gas in its atmosphere is what makes Neptune look blue.

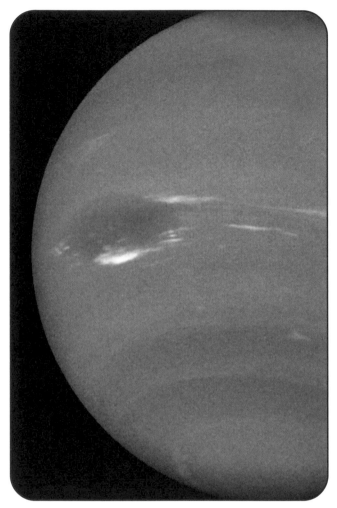

A white cloud scoots around Neptune every 16 hours or so. Scientists call it — what else? — "the scooter."

What would it be like to visit Neptune?

Because Neptune is so far from the Sun, it is freezing cold. The temperature in the tops of the clouds is about -175°C (-283°F). And it's windy. Blowing at speeds of up to 1120 km/h (700 m.p.h.), Neptune's winds are the fastest in the solar system.

Like Jupiter, Saturn and Uranus, Neptune is covered in a thick layer of gas. If you could penetrate it, you'd find yourself floating in an ocean of water, ammonia and methane.

Does Neptune have moons?

Neptune has 13 moons. Some are so small that scientists call them moonlets.

Neptune's biggest moon, Triton, is a strange place. It's the coldest body in the solar system and has a cracked, icy surface that looks like the skin of a cantaloupe. Its polar ice cap has volcanoes that erupt, spewing gas and dust 8 km (5 mi.) into the sky.

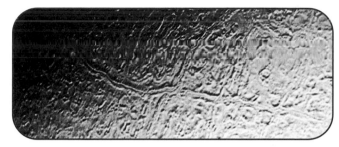

Is this a cantaloupe or is it Neptune's moon Triton? You're right if you guessed Triton.

NEPTUNE FACTS

- A Neptune year is 164.8 Earth years long. That's how long it takes Neptune to orbit the Sun.

- Neptune rotates on its axis once every 16 hours and 7 minutes.

- Neptune has four rings. Unlike the chunky rings of Uranus, Neptune's rings are made of tiny particles.

- Neptune was named after the Roman god of the sea because it is mostly liquid. Scientists think Neptune also has a small, rocky core.

- A space probe has passed closer to Neptune than any other planet. In 1989, *Voyager 2* cruised 4800 km (3000 mi.) above Neptune's cloud tops.

Pluto: The first dwarf planet

Pluto was called "the ninth planet" for over 75 years. Still, many scientists argued that the distant body was too small to be a true planet. They pointed out that Pluto's orbit is tilted and it has many close neighbors in the solar system. Finally, at a meeting in August 2006, astronomers decided to create a new category. Pluto became the very first "dwarf planet."

Pluto is the largest object in this photo taken by the Hubble Space Telescope. Slightly smaller Charon orbits around Pluto. The two tiny points of light in the photo are also moon-like objects. They were discovered in 2005, and have been named Nix and Hydra.

What would it be like to visit Pluto?

Don't expect a warm welcome after your long journey to Pluto. Even when the dwarf planet is at its closest to the Sun, the temperature is a bone-chilling -233°C (-387°F).

To explore Pluto's icy, rocky surface, you might want to bring along some extra weights. Your weight on Pluto would be one-twentieth of what it is on Earth. Without extra weights, each step would be like a high jump.

PLUTO FACTS

- A year on Pluto is 247.7 Earth years. That's how long it takes Pluto to orbit the Sun.

- Pluto rotates on its axis once every six days and nine hours.

- To learn more about distant Pluto, scientists have launched a space probe called *New Horizons*. The piano-sized probe is scheduled to reach Pluto in 2015, after traveling across the solar system for nine years.

- Pluto's thin atmosphere is made of nitrogen and carbon monoxide.

- Pluto was discovered in 1930 by Clyde Tombaugh at the Lowell Observatory in Flagstaff, Arizona. He was looking for a planet whose gravity might be pulling on Uranus and Neptune.

- Pluto's orbit is tilted compared to the paths of the planets.

- Pluto is smaller than our moon. It is one of about 800 objects in the Kuiper belt region of the solar system.

Try It!

Match postcards with planets

Al the Alien sent you postcards from his tour of the solar system. Trouble is, Al forgot to tell you which planet was which. Can you figure it out? (Answers on page 202.)

1 Today I saw a volcano three times higher than Earth's puny Mount Everest. Now I'm back in my spaceship trying to wash all the red dust off my antennae.

My Earthling Friends,
Planet Earth,
Solar System,
Milky Way Galaxy,
The Universe

2 Phew! That was a close call. My ship got sucked into a huge hurricane. Red clouds swirled around — I thought I would never get out alive.

My Earthling Friends,
Planet Earth,
Solar System,
Milky Way Galaxy,
The Universe

3 Help! My spaceship is being blown around in a blue-green fog. And the day is going on and on and on. Will the sun NEVER set?

My Earthling Friends,
Planet Earth,
Solar System,
Milky Way Galaxy,
The Universe

4 Hey – your moon astronauts would feel right at home here. It's got tons of craters and almost no air. Trouble is, while one side of the planet freezes, the other sizzles.

5 Choke! Gasp! No way I'm going down through those yellow clouds! My throat is burning and I feel like I've been roasted.

My Earthling Friends,
Planet Earth,
Solar System,
Milky Way Galaxy,
The Universe

6 This has got to be one fancy planet. You should see the rings! I mean, I saw thin bands around Jupiter, Neptune and Uranus but these ones beat them all.

My Earthling Friends,
Planet Earth,
Solar System,
Milky Way Galaxy,
The Universe

7 Today, for the first time, I saw trees. Amazing! I also spotted some birds, tigers, monkeys, flowers and dragonflies. This place is terrific — I hope people take care of it.

My Earthling Friends,
Planet Earth,
Solar System,
Milky Way Galaxy,
The Universe

Are there any more planets in our solar system?

No more solar system objects match the criteria for planets set by astronomers in 2006. However, several objects are similar in size and shape to the dwarf planet Pluto. For example, Ceres, the largest asteroid, and Eris, an object in the Kuiper belt, both match the description of a dwarf planet.

	How far is it from the sun?	What is its diameter?	How long does it take to rotate on its axis?*	How long does it take to orbit the sun?	How many moons does it have?	Does it have any rings?
MERCURY	58 million km (36 million mi.)	4879 km (3031 mi.)	58 days 14 hours	88 days	0	no
VENUS	108 million km (67 million mi.)	12 104 km (7521 mi.)	243 days 5 hours	224.7 days	0	no
EARTH	150 million km (93 million mi.)	12 756 km (7926 mi.)	23 hours 56 minutes	365.2 days	1	no
MARS	228 million km (142 million mi.)	6787 km (4217 mi.)	24 hours 37 minutes	687 days	2	no
JUPITER	778 million km (483 million mi.)	142 800 km (88 732 mi.)	9 hours 50 minutes	11.9 years	over 60	yes
SATURN	1427 million km (886 million mi.)	120 660 km (74 975 mi.)	10 hours 14 minutes	29.5 years	over 30	yes
URANUS	3 billion km (2 billion mi.)	51 118 km (31 763 mi.)	17 hours 14 minutes	84 years	over 25	yes
NEPTUNE	4 billion km (3 billion mi.)	49 528 km (30 775 mi.)	16 hours 7 minutes	164.8 years	13	yes

* On most planets, rotation time roughly equals one "day," the time from sunrise to sunrise. On Mercury, Venus and Uranus, however, rotation time does not equal a day. From one sunrise to the next on Mercury is 176 Earth days and on Venus, 117 Earth days. Because Uranus spins on its side, some parts of the planet are in darkness for 42 Earth years at a time.

Why study the planets?

People have always been curious about the planets. Some questions have been answered but many more remain. Scientists are still puzzled about what's inside the giant planets Jupiter, Saturn, Uranus and Neptune. They want to know if Venus has active volcanoes and if there is life on Mars. And they want to see if what has happened on other planets could happen to Earth. Learning about distant worlds helps us understand and take care of our own planet Earth.

13. The solar system: Comets, asteroids and meteorites

Rocks that drop from the sky. Strange lights that flash and glow. Craters that dent the ground. Long ago, people observed these things with wonder and fear. Today we know much more about comets, asteroids and meteorites. Here's what scientists tell us about these amazing — sometimes dangerous — space rocks.

What is a comet?

A comet is a ball of ice, gas and rocky dirt. It circles the Sun in a long, nearly oval path called an orbit. When a comet passes near the Sun, it develops a large, glowing head and a long tail. Bright comets can be seen easily from Earth.

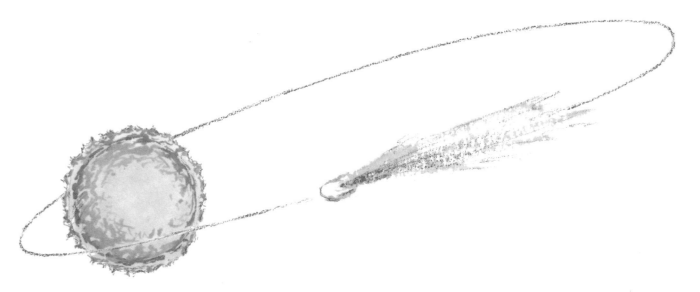

What is an asteroid?

An asteroid is a chunk of rock or metal that orbits the Sun. Most asteroids travel in a zone between the orbits of Mars and Jupiter, but some cross Earth's path. Asteroids are difficult to spot. Through a telescope, they look like tiny stars.

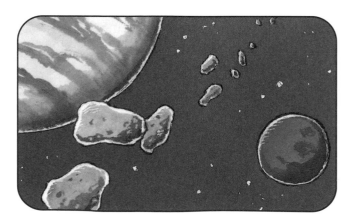

What is a meteorite?

Asteroids often collide with one another, scattering broken pieces in space. When one of these rocky fragments lands on Earth, it is called a meteorite.

Comets: The space travelers

A hazy ball of light glows eerily overhead. Night after night, it moves slowly and steadily across the dark sky. Long ago, people were frightened by these ghostly visitors, but today we know it is a comet making its long journey around the Sun.

In 1997, Comet Hale-Bopp glowed brightly with reflected sunlight for several weeks. Hale-Bopp will return in about 2400 years.

What do comets look like?

Most comets are too small and too far away to be seen from Earth. When a comet passes near the Sun, however, its glowing head makes it look much bigger and brighter in the night sky.

A bright comet is an amazing sight. It glows like a huge, hazy star with a long, ghostly tail.

Comet stories

In 1665, thousands of people in London, England, died of a terrible disease. The next year, fire nearly destroyed the city. Because two comets had just appeared in the sky, many people were convinced a comet meant disaster.

In ancient China, a comet's bushy tail reminded people of a broom. They said the gods used the comet to sweep away evil.

Comet Halley was gleaming as William the Conqueror prepared to invade England in 1066. Later the same year, William defeated Harold II at the Battle of Hastings. "The comet made us lose," said Harold's men.

A bright comet came into view shortly after Roman emperor Julius Caesar was murdered. Some said the comet was Caesar's soul, returning to haunt his enemies. Caesar's grandnephew and heir, Octavian, said the comet meant Caesar was a god.

What are comets made of?

Comets are often called "dirty snowballs." That's because each comet has a core — called its nucleus — that is made of dust, ice and frozen gases.

Each time a comet approaches the Sun, its frozen nucleus heats up. Gases and dust escape and surround the nucleus in a huge cloud called a coma. The Sun's energy pushes some of the comet's gas and dust into one or more long wispy tails.

If you built a model comet with a pea for the nucleus, your comet's coma would be as big as a football field. And the end of its tail might be 100 km (62 mi.) away!

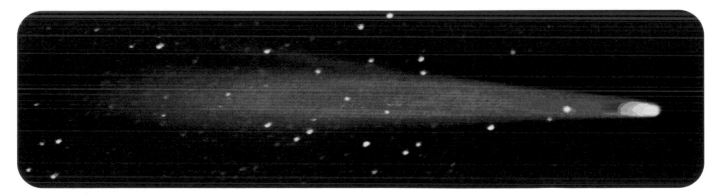

Comet Halley, one of the most famous comets, has fascinated people throughout history. Even though the comet shines so brightly, its nucleus is actually darker than coal.

Why do comets have tails?

Comets have two types of tails — gas tails and dust tails. Both types appear when a comet is near the Sun.

A gas tail usually points straight behind the comet. It forms when electrically charged particles from the Sun — the solar wind — blow on the comet's coma.

A dust tail often curves away from the comet's path. Escaping gases push dust off the head of the comet. Because the dust tail is made of solid particles, it has a different shape than the gas tail. Some comets have several dust tails and a gas tail, too.

Why do comet tails always point away from the Sun?

Comets' tails are blown outward from the Sun by the solar wind. Because a comet's tail is not caused by the comet's motion, it can even travel in front of the comet.

Comet Challenge: Can you tell from a comet's photo which way the comet is going? (Answer on page 202.)

The name "comet" comes from the Greek words *astro kometes*, which mean "long-haired star."

Where do comets come from?

Comets are leftover bits from the formation of the solar system. These icy objects cluster in at least two different places. Short-period comets — ones that orbit the Sun in less than 200 years — lie in the Kuiper belt. This ring of space objects also includes the dwarf planet Pluto.

Other comets surround the whole solar system in a huge swarm. This sphere of comets is called the Oort cloud after its discoverer, Jan Oort. The outer limits of the Oort cloud are 1000 times farther away from the Sun than Neptune and Pluto.

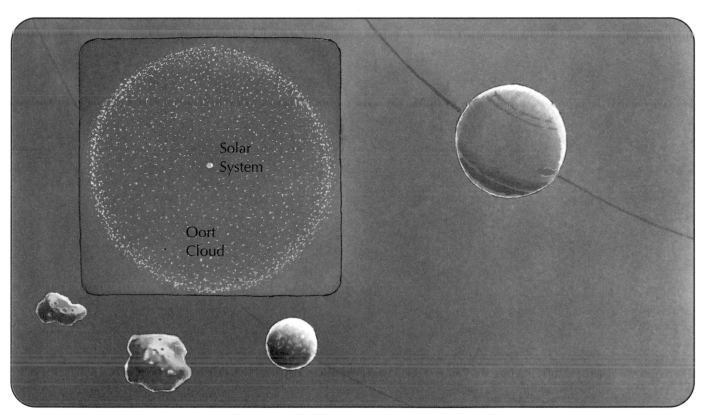

Solar
System

Oort
Cloud

What keeps a comet in orbit?

A comet is kept in its orbit by the Sun's strong pulling power, called gravity. Gravity also keeps Earth and the other planets circling the Sun.

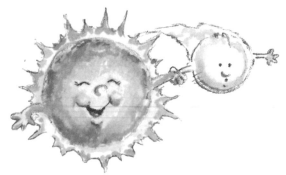

Does a comet's orbit ever change?

A comet sometimes leaves its home in the Kuiper belt or the Oort cloud to travel closer to the Sun. Scientists think a comet in the Oort cloud might be pulled into its new orbit by a passing star. A comet in the Kuiper belt could be tugged by the gravity of a larger object such as Neptune or Pluto.

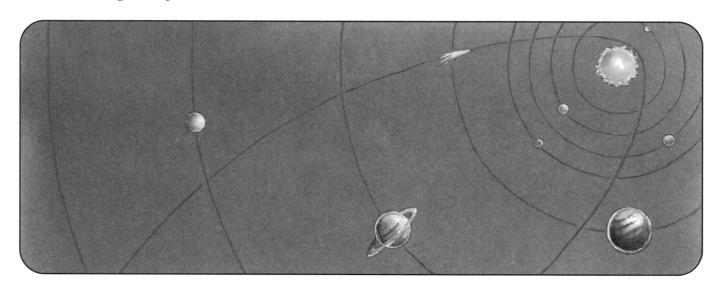

Why do comets appear to stay still?

Comets are very far away. So even though they zoom quickly through space, we don't notice their motion. (Think of watching a plane in the sky — even though it is traveling fast, it seems to move slowly when it is far away.) To see a comet move, you need to watch its position over several nights.

How fast are comets?

Comets travel around the Sun at about 160 000 km/h (100 000 m.p.h.). This makes them some of the fastest things in the solar system.

How long do comets last?

Every time a comet passes the Sun, it loses ice, gas and dust from its nucleus. After about 500 passes, all that's left is a rocky lump.

Instead of shrinking gradually, a comet may be destroyed when it crashes into a planet or the Sun. Or the gravity of a passing planet may cause it to fly out of the solar system, never to be seen again.

Some comets have been around for hundreds or thousands of years. Comet Halley was recorded by Chinese astronomers in 240 B.C., so it is at least 2000 years old.

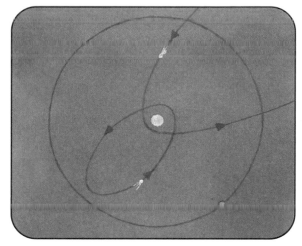

Comets with wide orbits usually last longer because they pass the Sun less often.

COMET FACTS

- A comet's tail is spread so thin that a huge sports arena full of tail material would contain less matter than a teaspoon of ordinary air.

- Comet West was so bright its head could be seen during the daytime in 1976.

- Caroline Herschel (1750–1848) was the first woman to discover a comet. She also helped her brother William discover the planet Uranus.

- The most frequent comet to orbit the Sun is Comet Encke. It passes around the Sun every 3.3 years.

- A comet's nucleus is a few kilometers (miles) across. Its coma is much wider — about 100 000 km (62 000 mi.). A comet's tail is amazingly long. It can stretch hundreds of millions of kilometers (miles).

Who made the first comet prediction?

In 1682, Edmond Halley watched a brilliant comet blaze in the sky over England. Then he figured out that two earlier comets had traced the same path. Each comet had followed the other by about 75 years.

Halley realized he was not studying three separate comets — just one that kept coming back. "It should return again around the year 1758," he wrote to a friend.

Halley's prediction came true in early 1759, and the comet was named after him. Comet Halley still reappears about every 75 years.

How do scientists predict comets?

Astronomers have used old records of comet sightings to identify about 180 comets with orbits shorter than 200 years. They also search the sky with powerful telescopes to find comets that are still a long way from Earth.

When a comet appears, scientists begin to measure its position. They need at least three different measurements to calculate the rest of its orbit.

But not all comets behave in ways that scientists expect. Sometimes an expected comet doesn't turn up, or it looks different from what was predicted. When Comet Halley returned in 1986, many people were disappointed because it wasn't very bright.

How are new comets discovered?

Comet hunters scan the night sky with telescopes, looking for anything unusual. Sometimes they find a fuzzy spot of light that isn't on the star maps. Right away, they contact other astronomers. Why the rush? If the new spot turns out to be a comet, it will be named after the one or two people who reported it first.

What have space probes discovered about comets?

Two space probes visited Comet Halley in 1986. They revealed that the comet's nucleus is a lumpy mixture of ice and rock about 16 km (10 mi.) across. In 2006, the space probe *Stardust* returned from a seven-year journey into space. *Stardust* captured images of the pit-marked nucleus of Comet Wild 2 (pronounced Vilt 2) and collected dust from its coma. By analyzing this ancient space dust, scientists can learn more about the beginnings of our solar system.

What happens when a comet hits a planet?

In July 1994, astronomers around the world pointed their telescopes at Jupiter. The giant planet was about to be hit by Comet Shoemaker-Levy 9, but no one could predict the size of the impact. On July 16, the comet plunged into Jupiter's foggy atmosphere. Some of the comet's 20 fragments produced huge gas geysers and explosions. Others left gigantic bruises. One dark splotch was wider than Earth. In a few days, Jupiter's rapid rotation turned the round scar into a dark band that circled the planet. The streak lasted for several months before it faded away.

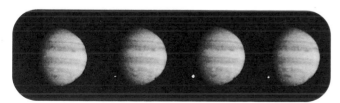

These images, taken 2⅓ seconds apart, show a fragment of Comet Shoemaker-Levy 9 colliding with Jupiter.

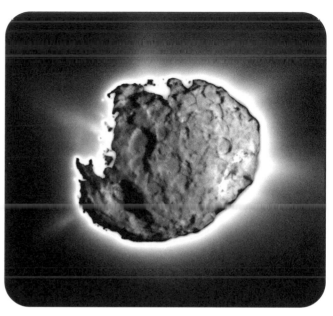

This is an image of the four-kilometer (2.5 mi.) nucleus of Comet Wild 2.

Will a comet ever collide with Earth?

About 500 comets cross Earth's orbit as they travel around the Sun. Luckily, none of these comets appear to be on a collision course with Earth. Comets have bumped into Earth in the past and they will again, but the chances of a large impact happening in your lifetime are very small.

Bits of comet dust collide with Earth's atmosphere all the time. They usually burn up and can be seen as bright flashes of light called meteors, or shooting stars.

147

Try It!

Learn more about the craters on the Moon

Comets and asteroids have crashed into the planets — and even into our Moon — again and again. Check out the Moon and see the deep, wide craters left by these impacts.

YOU WILL NEED

- high-power binoculars
- a clear night with a first or last quarter Moon (When the Moon is partially lit up, deep shadows help you see craters more clearly.)
- a reclining lawn chair
- the Moon map on this page

1 Hold the binoculars steady by resting your elbows on the arms of the lawn chair. You may need to lay a board across the arms of the chair to make a comfortable support.

2 Focus the binoculars on the Moon's surface. Compare what you see with the Moon map. Hold the map so that it lines up with your view of the Moon.

3 The large dark areas are flatlands where lava flooded the Moon billions of years ago. They are called "maria" — seas — even though they contain no water. Look for craters in the areas between the maria.

4 Take a close look at the Tycho, Copernicus or Stevinus craters. Can you see the rays spreading from them? These rays are the patterns that formed when rock splashed out during a huge comet or asteroid impact.

Comet Challenge: Why do we see so many craters on the Moon and so few on Earth? (Answer on page 202.)

First Quarter

Last Quarter

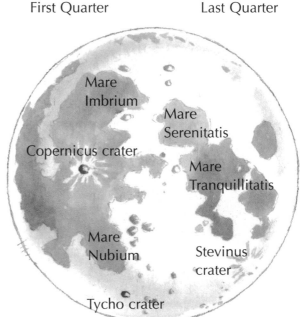

Mare Imbrium

Mare Serenitatis

Copernicus crater

Mare Tranquillitatis

Mare Nubium

Stevinus crater

Tycho crater

Asteroids: Mini-planets

Most of the time, asteroids float harmlessly in space, traveling in wide rings between the orbits of Mars and Jupiter. Sometimes, two asteroids collide and break into smaller pieces. And once in a long while, an asteroid plunges toward Earth — with results that can be disastrous.

Asteroid Eros is about 33 km (20 mi.) long. Eros is covered with craters formed when other asteroids crashed into its surface.

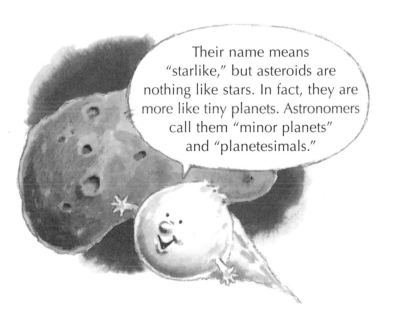

Their name means "starlike," but asteroids are nothing like stars. In fact, they are more like tiny planets. Astronomers call them "minor planets" and "planetesimals."

How did asteroids form?

About 4.5 billion years ago, our solar system began from a huge, swirling cloud of gas and dust particles. The particles clumped together, forming the Sun and many smaller objects. Planets took shape when these small objects smashed together. After the planets formed, thousands of rocky bits were left over. Today we call them asteroids.

A deadly impact

A large asteroid — or possibly a comet — smashed into Earth 65 million years ago. It may have destroyed the last of the dinosaurs.

Many scientists believe the scene was something like this: While Triceratops munched giant ferns, and Tyrannosaurus rex munched Triceratops, an asteroid hurtled toward Earth. It measured 12 km (7 mi.) across and dropped 300 times faster than a bullet shot from a gun.

The asteroid hit Earth with a crash that blasted a huge crater. Bits of burning rock flew off in all directions. Wherever the rocks landed, fires began.

Smoke from the fires and dust from the crash soon filled the air above the impact site. Within hours it blew around the whole planet and darkened the sky.

Without sunlight, most plants could not live. Animals had little to eat. Over time, all of the dinosaurs and many other animals became extinct. They had been killed by a visitor from outer space.

What are asteroids made of?

Most asteroids are made of rock. They are called stony asteroids. Some asteroids are made of iron, nickel and other metals. They are called iron asteroids. A few asteroids are made of a combination of rock and metal. They are known as the "stony-irons."

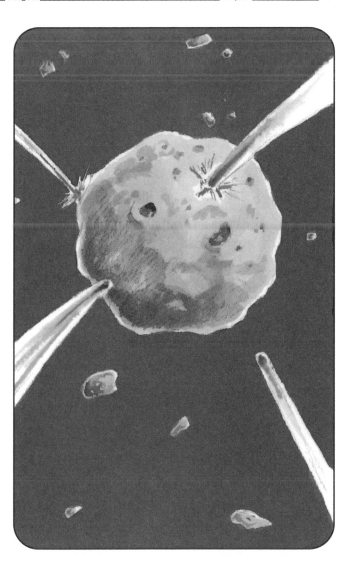

This close-up of the asteroid Gaspra was taken by the *Galileo* space probe. Gaspra is a stony asteroid.

How is an asteroid different from a planet?

Asteroids are much smaller than planets and are shaped differently. Most asteroids do not have enough gravity to pull them into well-formed spheres. Instead of being shaped like a grapefruit, the average asteroid looks more like a lumpy baked potato.

Try It!

Make a reflector detector

YOU WILL NEED

- a medium-sized cardboard box
- black construction paper
- tape
- a mini-flashlight (one that takes AA batteries)
- a variety of old and new coins, including pennies, nickels, dimes and quarters

1 Lay the cardboard box on its side on a table so the opening is facing you.

2 Tape the black paper inside the box on the rear wall.

3 Place the flashlight inside the box, facing toward you and away from the black paper. Turn on the flashlight.

4 Hold one coin at a time in the flashlight's beam. Move the coin around until you see a spot of reflected light on the black paper.

5 Compare the light reflected by different coins. Can you find a dime that reflects more light than a quarter? Can you pick out a penny by its reflected light alone?

Like your coins, some asteroids reflect more light than others. Depending on its surface material, a small asteroid may be brighter than an asteroid twice its size. For example, Vesta, the fourth-largest asteroid, is brighter than Ceres, the largest asteroid of all.

How big are asteroids?

Ceres, the largest asteroid, is big enough to be considered a dwarf planet. It measures 930 km (578 mi.) across and would almost cover an area the size of Alaska. Next comes Pallas at about half that size. Pallas would cover Arizona. Altogether, astronomers have found about 200 asteroids wider than 100 km (62 mi.), but most are much smaller. Some are no bigger than a house.

Where are asteroids found?

Most asteroids circle the Sun in a series of rings called the main belt. This wide, flat band lies between the orbits of Mars and Jupiter. Unlike the asteroid-packed zone you might see in science-fiction movies, the main asteroid belt has plenty of empty space between asteroids. In fact, spacecraft traveling to Jupiter and beyond have passed through the asteroid belt unharmed.

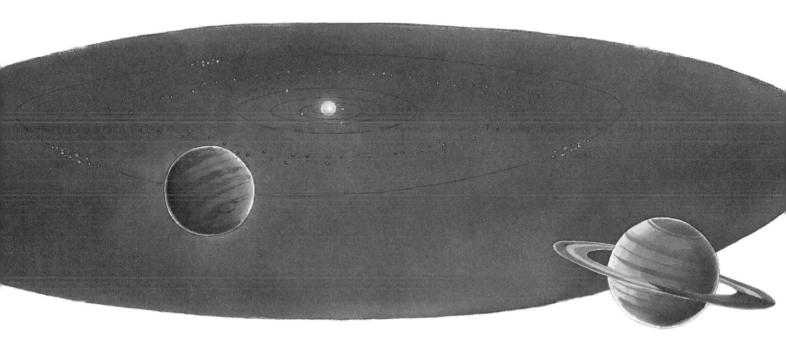

Do asteroids ever leave their orbits?

Asteroids sometimes crash into each other. These collisions can knock pieces out of the asteroid belt and into new orbits.

Some asteroids, called the Trojans, travel along the same path as Jupiter. Others, called the Amors, cross the orbit of Mars. Asteroids called the Apollos regularly cross the orbit of Earth.

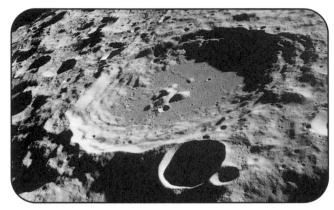

The Moon shows the scars of countless comet and asteroid impacts.

How were asteroids discovered?

In 1800, astronomers believed that most planets were evenly spaced apart. They wondered why there was such a large gap between the orbits of Mars and Jupiter. Was there a missing planet?

In 1801, an Italian monk named Giuseppe Piazzi discovered a tiny object orbiting the Sun between Mars and Jupiter. He named it Ceres after the Roman goddess of grain.

But Ceres was too small to be a planet. Astronomers agreed to call it an asteroid because it looked like a small star through their telescopes. Within a few years, several more asteroids were found.

Does anything live on asteroids?

As far as we know, nothing lives on asteroids. However, some asteroids contain water, carbon and other compounds necessary for life. Life on Earth may have started when asteroids carried these compounds to our planet billions of years ago.

ASTEROID FACTS

- If you could lump together all the asteroids in the asteroid belt, you would have a ball smaller than our Moon.

- Vesta is the brightest of all the asteroids. If you know exactly where to look, it can be seen with binoculars.

- Small asteroids often pass closer to Earth than the distance from Earth to the Moon.

- About 5000 asteroids have been given official names and numbers. Asteroids 3350 to 3356 are named after the astronauts who died when the space shuttle *Challenger* exploded.

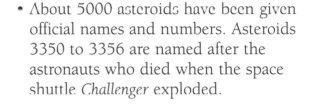

- The planet Mars has two moons, Phobos and Deimos (page 119). These small, bumpy moons may be asteroids that have been captured by the gravity of Mars.

How do scientists study asteroids?

Even through telescopes, asteroids look like tiny dots of light. Still, astronomers are able to figure out what asteroids are made of by analyzing their reflected light.

In 2001, the Near-Earth Asteroid Rendezvous (NEAR) mission made history when it explored the asteroid Eros. The NEAR spacecraft, *Shoemaker*, was the first to orbit an asteroid and touch down on its surface.

An earlier space probe, *Galileo*, took the very first asteroid photos in 1991. It showed that the asteroid Gaspra was a rocky lump covered with craters. The *Galileo* probe also sent back portraits of the asteroid Ida. Scientists were surprised to see Ida has its own mini-moon!

Will an asteroid hit Earth?

Asteroids have crashed into Earth in the past and will hit our planet in the future. A few astronomers are studying near-Earth asteroids so they can predict the next big impact.

In March 1998, astronomers announced that an enormous asteroid might collide with Earth in 2028. Fortunately, the astronomers changed their prediction a few days later. Based on new data, they decided that the asteroid will pass Earth at a safe distance. Phew!

If an asteroid is detected heading for Earth, rockets and explosives might be used to push it away from our planet.

Try It!

Compare hard-hitting asteroids

Imagine two same-sized asteroids zipping toward Earth at the same speed. Which would hit with greater force — the one made of stone or the one made of metal? See for yourself in this activity.

YOU WILL NEED

- a stone about half the size of a tennis ball
- a measuring cup
- water
- about 200 pennies
- two small yogurt containers

Step one: Match volumes of stone and metal

1 Place the stone in the measuring cup. Pour in enough water to reach the 250 mL (1 c.) mark.

2 Carefully remove the stone from the cup. Notice how much the water level drops. The difference in level shows the volume of the missing stone.

3 Add enough pennies to replace the stone's volume. Stop when the water again reaches the 250 mL (1 c.) mark.

4 Drain the water. Pour the pennies into one yogurt container and place the stone in the other. Like two same-sized asteroids, your containers now hold matching volumes of stone and metal.

Step two: Compare the mass

Hold the container with the stone in one hand. Pick up the container with the pennies in your other hand. Which container is heavier?

Like your samples, a metal asteroid is heavier — and has more mass — than a stone asteroid the same size. In a head-on collision with Earth, the metal asteroid would produce a greater crash.

Meteorites: Stones from the sky

Scientists believe that this iron meteorite is a small piece from the core of a large asteroid that broke apart.

Every day, rocky invaders from outer space crash through Earth's atmosphere. The smaller ones burn up, leaving fiery trails of light called meteors. Larger pieces — meteorites — crash onto the ground. For centuries, people have been scared and excited about these rocks from space.

About 40 000 years ago, a house-sized iron meteorite slammed into the Arizona desert and left a huge hole called Meteor Crater. The crater floor is so large, it could hold 20 football fields.

Stories from the past

In many parts of Europe, people used to say that a meteor meant someone had died.

Native people of northern California said meteors were the souls of their leaders traveling to life after death.

In many parts of the world, people say you should make a wish when you see a meteor.

Ancient Egyptians did not know how to get iron from the ground. The only iron they had came from meteorites. People gave a special name to the rare metal they used for tools and weapons. They called it "stone of heaven."

The ancient Greeks placed an especially large meteorite in a sacred temple. They said it was the goddess Artemis, who had fallen from the sky.

Old German stories told of meteorites containing many strange things. In some stories meteorites carried messages from the dead; in others they held ham, rotten cheese, silver, gold and money.

What is the difference between a meteoroid, a meteor and a meteorite?

A meteoroid is a small chunk of space debris left behind by a passing comet or asteroid.

A meteor is the streak of light you see when a meteoroid burns up as it falls through Earth's atmosphere.

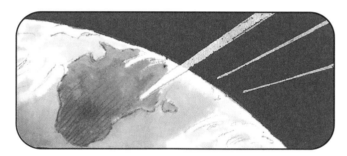

A meteorite is a meteoroid that survives its fall through the atmosphere and lands on Earth's surface.

Why are meteors so bright?

When a small meteoroid speeds into Earth's atmosphere, it may be traveling faster than a bullet from a gun. The air ahead of it quickly becomes so squished and heated that it glows. For a second or two, a meteor flashes across the sky. Incredible as it seems, some of the brightest meteors are produced by meteoroids no bigger than a grape.

Meteors are sometimes called "shooting stars," or "falling stars," even though they aren't stars at all.

What are meteorites made of?

Meteorites are made of metal or rock, or a combination of the two materials. Most meteorites are pieces of asteroids that break off when two asteroids collide.

The rock in an asteroid-type meteorite is as old as the solar system. If a meteorite is made of younger rock, scientists know it was probably thrown off the Moon or Mars during a major collision with an asteroid or comet.

Tiny meteorites, called micrometeorites, float down to Earth as dust. Because they are so light, they don't travel fast enough to burn up in the atmosphere. Most of them come from the tail of a passing comet. Every year, 40 000 t (44 000 tn) of micrometeorite material lands on Earth.

Meteorites that are spotted as they crash down are called "falls." Meteorites found on the ground are called "finds."

On October 9, 1992, Michelle Knapp heard a crash outside her home in Peekskill, New York. She discovered that her car had been hit by a football-sized meteorite.

What are meteor showers?

Meteor showers are displays of many meteors in one night. They happen when Earth passes through the dust trail left behind by a comet. Earth crosses several comet trails each year as it orbits around the Sun, so famous meteor showers are seen at the same time year after year.

What is a fireball?

A fireball is an extra-bright meteor produced when a large meteoroid plunges toward Earth. Some fireballs are so bright that they can be seen during the daytime. They are often accompanied by a series of loud bangs or thundering sounds. Some even explode in the sky.

A meteor shower won't get you clean. But it will give you a chance to see dozens of meteors in one night.

In 1908, a huge fireball exploded over a remote part of Siberia. People over 900 km (600 mi.) away heard the boom. It flattened trees for 32 km (20 mi.) around. The explosion was much greater than the 1980 eruption of the Mount St. Helens volcano.

Try It!

Watch a meteor shower

YOU WILL NEED

- a calendar that shows the Moon's phases
- a clear night with no Full Moon
- a place with a wide-open view of the sky
- warm clothes
- an adult's permission to stay up really late

Meteor showers happen when Earth passes through dust left behind by a comet. Several showers can be seen regularly year after year. They are named after the constellations they appear to come from.

Here are names and dates* of the best meteor showers:

Quadrantids	January 3
Eta Aquarids	May 6
Perseids	August 12
Orionids	October 21
Leonids	November 16
Geminids	December 13

* You also might see meteor showers on the nights just before and after these dates.

1 Check out the meteor shower dates on your calendar. Look for showers that will happen when there is a New or Crescent Moon. Plan to do some sky watching on those nights.

2 Go out as late as possible. The Geminid shower can be seen around 10 p.m., but most meteor showers are better after midnight, when your side of Earth is heading directly into the comet dust trail.

3 Avoid bright lights so your eyes will get used to the dark. If the weather is warm enough, lie down on a lawn chair or blanket for a more comfortable view.

4 Patiently scan the sky. You are watching for bright streaks of light that last about one second. On a dark, clear night you might see a meteor every minute or two. If you are near city lights or if the Moon is bright, meteors will be harder to see.

What happens when a meteorite hits Earth?

Tiny micrometeorites fall to Earth all the time and we don't even notice them. Larger chunks of rock may land in the ocean or desert and never be observed. But sometimes a meteorite landing can't be ignored.

Mrs. Elizabeth Hodges was badly bruised when a meteorite crashed through the roof of her Alabama home in 1954. Mrs. Hodges is the only person known to have been hit by a meteorite.

METEORITE FACTS

- The largest meteorite in the world fell in southwestern Africa. Its estimated weight is over 50 t (55 tn).

- A dog was killed by a meteorite that fell in Egypt in 1911. Scientists figured out that the rock had come all the way from Mars.

- On April 26, 1803, thousands of small meteorites rained down on a town near Paris, France.

- NASA scientists are studying a meteorite that formed on Mars and landed in Antarctica. The meteorite might hold microscopic fossils. Scientists are asking, "Was there once life on Mars?"

Try It!

See how meteorites impact Earth

Watch what happens when a meteorite strikes the ground. This activity can be messy, so ask an adult's permission before you begin.

YOU WILL NEED

- a large plastic bucket
- 500 mL (2 c.) flour
- 50 mL (1/4 c.) cocoa powder
- a sifter
- old newspapers
- 3 marbles

1 Spread the flour in the bottom of the bucket. Make it as smooth as possible.

2 Sift the cocoa to cover the surface of the flour.

3 Spread the newspapers on the floor and place the bucket on top of them.

4 Drop the marbles one at a time into the bucket.

5 Carefully remove the marbles and inspect your craters.

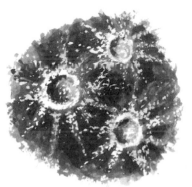

When a large meteorite hits Earth or the Moon, it splatters rock in all directions. The crater it produces often has a raised rim. Can you see these features in your craters?

165

Why study comets, asteroids and meteorites?

Although they come from outer space, comets, asteroids and meteorites can help us understand our world. Scientists are trying to answer many questions. Did comets bring water to our planet? How often have asteroids collided with Earth? Does a meteorite from Mars tell about ancient life on that planet?

Asteroids could be useful as refueling stations for space travelers, or as mines for precious minerals. By tracking comets and asteroids, we might be able to save ourselves from a disastrous collision.

We have learned many things about comets, asteroids and meteorites, but many more questions remain unanswered. Astronomers will continue their quest to learn more about these fascinating space rocks.

14. Diamonds in the sky: The stars

Stare up at the sky on a dark, clear night. The stars you see have dazzled sky watchers for thousands of years. Although we've learned a lot about the stars, many mysteries remain.

A star story

For centuries, people have told stories to explain the stars. This tale from India tells how the brightest star of all appeared in the sky.

Long, long ago, five princes set out to find the gateway to heaven. The eldest prince, Yudistira, brought his dog on the difficult journey.

One by one, the four younger princes gave up the quest and returned home. Only Yudistira hiked on, with his faithful dog trotting at his heels. He finally reached the foot of Mount Meru, where he was startled by a booming voice coming from the mountaintop.

"You have reached the gateway to heaven," said the god Indra. "Enter and find total happiness."

"May I bring my dog?" asked Yudistira. "He's my one true friend."

"No dogs allowed in heaven," said Indra. "That is the rule."

"Then we're both going home," said Yudistira. He called his dog and turned back down the mountain path. They were halfway back to the village when Yudistira heard the booming voice again.

"Come back!" called Indra. "Your love for each other has changed my mind. You and the dog are welcome here."

To celebrate their arrival in heaven, Indra arranged several stars in the shape of a dog. At its heart you can still see the Dog Star, today known as Sirius. It is the brightest star that can be seen in the sky.

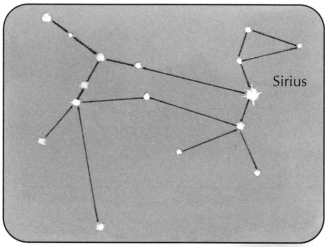

The Great Dog constellation

168

What is a star?

A star is a superhot ball of gases. The center of a star is like a huge nuclear furnace. There, hydrogen gas turns into helium, giving off enormous amounts of energy. We see some of this energy as light and feel some of it as heat.

Is the Sun a star?

Yes, our Sun is an ordinary, medium-sized star. It seems so big and bright because it is much closer to us than any other star. Earth and eight other planets circle around the Sun.

The Sun is so big that a million Earths could fit inside it. Still, it is just a medium-sized star.

169

Try It!

Cook with the Sun's rays

1 Cut one side out of the shoe box. Ask an adult to help you poke a hole in both ends as shown.

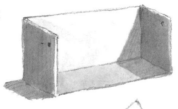

2 Cut two ends about the size shown out of the leftover piece of box or the lid. Poke holes as shown.

3 Attach the foil to the ends with tape. The shiny side of the foil should face in.

4 Set up your solar cooker as shown. Put it outside facing directly toward the Sun. Turn the hot dog or sausage every 10 minutes or so.

Like other stars, the Sun gives off huge amounts of energy. Some energy can be seen as light; some can be felt as heat. Does your solar cooker gather enough of the Sun's heat energy to heat up the hot dog or sausage?

How many stars are there?

On a clear, moonless night, far from the city lights, you can see about 2000 stars. That's a lot, but scientists tell us that the universe holds not just thousands or millions, or even billions, but *trillions* of stars. That's more than 1 000 000 000 000 stars!

A scientist who studies the stars is called an astronomer. In Greek, *astron* means star.

Do other stars have planets?

Astronomers have discovered many planetlike objects around distant stars. Although they can't see these objects directly, scientists use clues to find them. Sometimes an orbiting object pulls on its star and makes it wobble. Other times, an object crosses in front of a star and dims its light.

STAR FACTS

- Stars are not pure white. Cooler stars are slightly red or orange, while hotter stars are blue-white. Our Sun is a medium-hot yellow star.

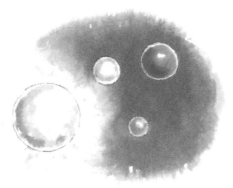

- Many stars come in pairs. These "binary stars" are held together by gravity.

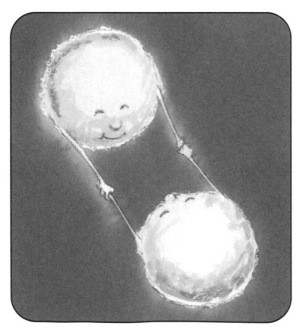

- Stars vary in size. Some would hold millions of Suns. Others are smaller than our Moon.

- The largest star you can see with your bare eyes is Betelgeuse. This supergiant star has a diameter 700 times that of the Sun.

This image of Betelgeuse was taken by the Hubble Space Telescope.

How is a star different from a planet?

A star glows with heat and light from the nuclear reactions in its core. Planets only appear to shine because they reflect the light from a star, our Sun.

A star is much hotter than a planet.

What is a shooting star?

Shooting stars aren't stars. They are meteors — brilliant streaks of light produced when particles of space dust burn up in Earth's atmosphere. A meteor particle is usually smaller than a pea. Still, it blazes a bright, fiery trail across the night sky.

How far away are the stars?

Our nearest star, the Sun, is 150 million km (93 million mi.) away. That's almost next door compared to other stars. Our next closest star is Proxima Centauri. It's about 40 trillion km (25 trillion mi.) away — 280 000 times as far as the Sun.

How do scientists measure space?

To measure the vast distances between stars, scientists use a special unit called a light-year. This is the distance light travels in one year. Because light is so speedy, one light-year is a long, long way — about 9.5 trillion km (6 trillion mi.). Proxima Centauri, the star closest to our solar system, is 4.2 light-years away.

If a star is 100 light-years away, the light you see tonight left the star 100 years ago. So when you gaze at distant stars, you're really looking back in time.

15. Seeing stars

To ancient people, the night sky was like a giant join-the-dots puzzle. They saw objects, animals, gods and people in the arrangement of the stars. Today, we call these patterns constellations. With a little practice, you too can see pictures in the sky.

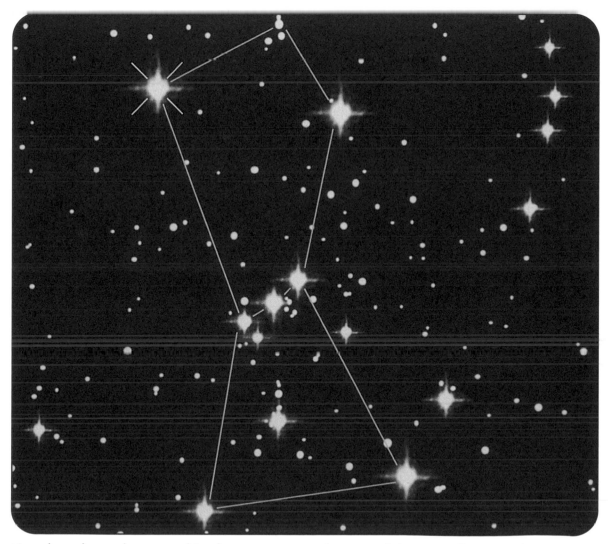

Lines have been drawn on this photo to connect the stars of the constellation Orion.

Orion, the great hunter

The ancient Greeks named one constellation after their hero, Orion. This is the story of how Orion came to be in the sky.

Artemis, the goddess of hunting, could hit any target with an arrow. When she met the great hunter Orion, she fell deeply in love.

But Apollo, the twin brother of Artemis, was jealous. How could he get rid of his sister's new friend?

Artemis broke her bow in fury. With tears running down her cheeks, she scooped Orion's body from the waves.

"You will never be forgotten," the goddess murmured as she lifted Orion into the heavens. To this day, you can spot Orion's sword, shield and belt shining in the sky.

One day, Apollo saw his chance. Orion was swimming far out at sea. Apollo called his sister down to the beach.

"I bet you can't hit that black rock," he said, pointing to Orion.

"Of course I can," replied Artemis. She loaded her bow, pulled back the string and took aim. Zing! The arrow flew through the air and pierced its target. For a moment, Artemis was proud and happy. Then Apollo told her that she had just killed Orion.

What is the Big Dipper?

The Big Dipper is a pattern of seven bright stars seen in the northern hemisphere. The stars form the shape of a long-handled pot like the ones used to dip water from a pail. In Britain, people call this same star pattern the Plough.

Though it is often called a constellation, the Big Dipper is actually just one part of a constellation called Ursa Major, or the Great Bear.

What is the North Star?

The North Star isn't especially bright, but it is important. It seems to stand still above the North Pole. Sailors long ago used it to help them navigate.

If you live in the northern hemisphere, you can find the North Star just by looking at the Big Dipper. Just follow a line through the two stars of the Dipper's outer edge.

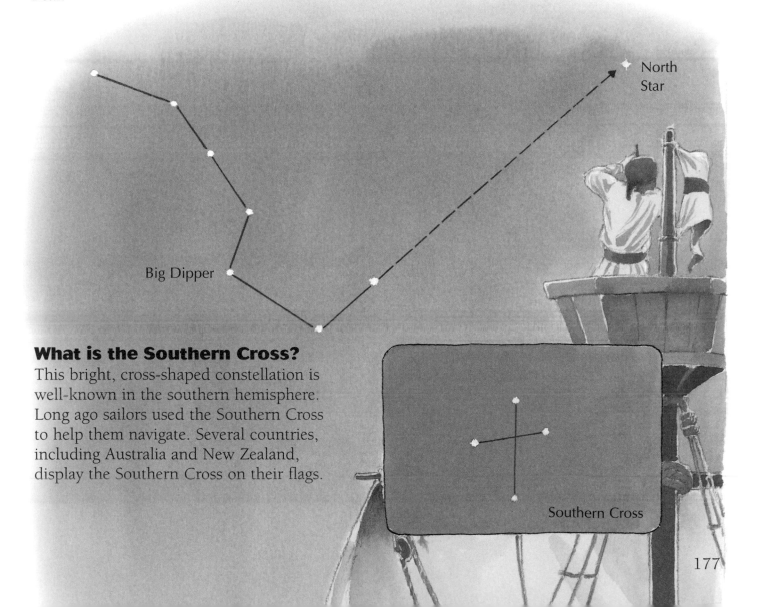

North Star

Big Dipper

What is the Southern Cross?

This bright, cross-shaped constellation is well-known in the southern hemisphere. Long ago sailors used the Southern Cross to help them navigate. Several countries, including Australia and New Zealand, display the Southern Cross on their flags.

Southern Cross

177

 ## Try It!

Make a model of the constellation Cygnus

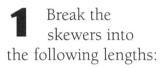

1 Break the skewers into the following lengths:

A: 29 cm (11 3/8 in.)
B: 19 cm (7 1/2 in.)
C: 2 cm (3/4 in.)
D: 10 cm (4 in.)
E: 30 cm (11 3/4 in.)
F: 10 cm (4 in.)

2 Stand each skewer piece in a modeling clay base. Top each with a small ball of aluminum foil. Scratch the letter for each skewer on the modeling clay base.

3 Lay a piece of paper over this page and trace the purple stars. Add their letters.

4 Lay the paper on a table and set each star on its matching letter. Fold the cardboard and stand it behind your model.

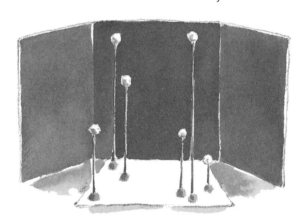

5 Look at your model from the front. Can you see a cross? Now look at your model from the side. As you can see, some stars are closer than others. In fact, some stars in Cygnus are more than 1000 light-years apart.

STAR FACTS

- Astronomers recognize 88 constellations.

- Castor and Pollux, the two brightest stars in the constellation Gemini, were named after a famous pair of twins. According to Greek myth, the twin boys were the sons of Leda, queen of Sparta, and the god Zeus.

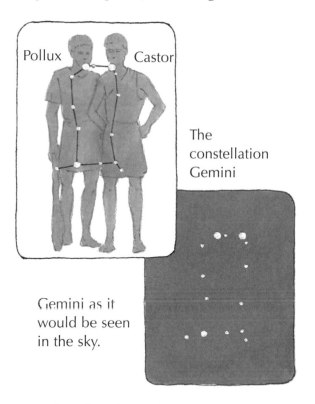

Pollux   Castor

The constellation Gemini

Gemini as it would be seen in the sky.

- A Cherokee legend says the stars in the handle of the Big Dipper are a band of hunters chasing the Great Bear across the sky.

- People call this constellation Leo the Lion. Does it look like a lion lying on the African plains?

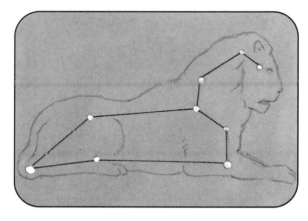

- For 5000 years, the constellation Taurus has been seen as a charging bull. Can you imagine the bull's horns?

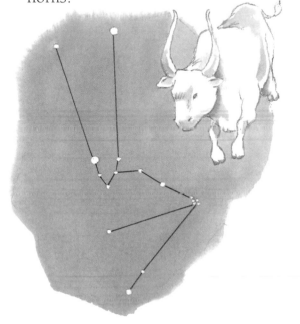

Try It!

Make a starry slide show

YOU WILL NEED

- a shoe box with a lid
- black poster paint
- a paintbrush
- scissors
- a sharp pencil
- a sheet of black bristol board
- 5 sheets of white paper
- glue
- a pin

To make the viewer:

1 Paint the inside of the shoe box and lid black.

2 Cut a rectangle out of one end of the shoe box. Leave a frame 2 cm (3/4 in.) around the sides and bottom.

3 With a pencil, pierce a peephole in the other end of the shoe box.

To make the slides:

1 Cut five rectangles of black bristol board to fit the open end of the shoe box. Cut five pieces of white paper the same size.

2 Draw five constellations on the white paper. Use the constellations from pages 178–182 as a guide.

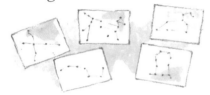

3 Glue one constellation drawing onto each black rectangle.

4 With the pin, poke a hole for each star in the constellation. For larger stars, make bigger holes.

Place one slide at a time into the end of your viewer. Look through the peephole while you hold the other end of your viewer toward a bright light. Can you name each constellation?

Why can't we see stars during the day?

Stars are always there in the sky. We can't see them during the day because the Sun's light makes the sky too bright. The same thing happens if you shine a flashlight in a bright room — you can't see the beam of light. But in the dark, there it is, shining brightly.

Why do stars twinkle?

The light from a star travels a long way to reach Earth. By the time it gets close to Earth, it is like a narrow beam. Particles in Earth's atmosphere, the blanket of air around our planet, bounce the light around. This makes the star appear to twinkle.

Why do some stars look brighter than others?

Some stars look bright because they're big. Others look bright because they're closer to us. Scientists call a star's brightness its magnitude. Apparent magnitude tells how bright the star looks from Earth. Absolute magnitude tells how bright the star really is compared to other stars.

Are the stars moving?

The stars seem to move slowly across the sky every night. Watching them, you might think that the stars are circling around us. But they're not — they only appear to move because the Earth is spinning.

Also, because the Earth travels around the Sun each year, the stars seem to change position from season to season. Actually, Earth's travels just give us a different view of the sky in summer, fall, winter and spring. So we can't see any real movement in the stars from day to day or month to month.

However, if we could watch the stars over many thousands of years, changes in their positions would be noticeable. That's because the stars are actually traveling through space.

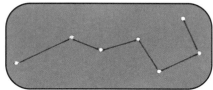

The Big Dipper 50 000 years ago

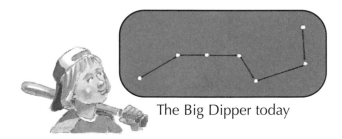

The Big Dipper today

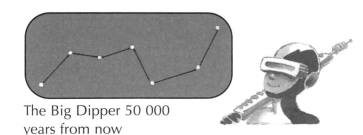

The Big Dipper 50 000 years from now

Try It!

Check out the night sky

YOU WILL NEED

- a clear night
- an open space away from bright lights
- an old blanket
- a flashlight with the lens covered with red tissue paper
- the constellation pictures from this chapter

1 Spread your blanket on the ground.

2 Use the flashlight to check the constellation pictures. The red tissue paper helps keep your eyes adjusted to the dark.

3 Look for the brightest stars in the sky. These stars are usually found in major constellations. Remember that the major constellations cover large areas of the sky.

Constellations are in different parts of the sky at different times of the year. To find out what you can expect to see this month, check the star charts in an astronomy magazine or on the Internet.

How do scientists study the stars?

Astronomers use telescopes on the Earth and in space to study the stars. They study the stars' visible light (the light we can see) and invisible light energy (such as radio waves and infrared radiation we can't see).

The light from each star can be split into a pattern called a spectrum. By studying a star's spectrum, scientists can figure out how hot the star is, what it is made of and how fast it is moving.

The Infrared Astronomical Satellite (IRAS) was put into orbit in 1983. It picks up infrared energy, a part of starlight we can't see.

What is the Hubble Space Telescope?

Imagine looking up at the sky from the bottom of a lake. That's pretty much what happens when we observe the stars through Earth's atmosphere. To get a clearer picture, scientists have sent telescopes into orbit beyond Earth's atmosphere.

The most famous of these is the Hubble Space Telescope. It was launched into orbit in 1990. At first, Hubble didn't work very well because of problems with its mirrors. Then, in 1993, it was repaired during a special space mission. Since then, the Hubble has been sending incredible star portraits back to Earth.

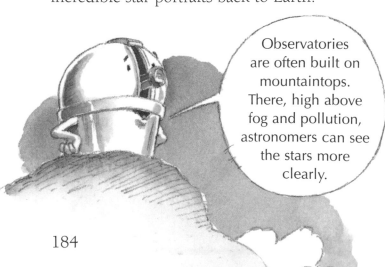

Observatories are often built on mountaintops. There, high above fog and pollution, astronomers can see the stars more clearly.

The Hubble Space Telescope is almost the size of a large school bus.

184

Try It!

Split a star's light

1 Set the mirror inside the glass so that it is resting at an angle.

2 Fill the glass with water.

3 Place the glass and mirror in a sunny window.

4 Move the glass until the mirror reflects sunlight onto the ceiling. You will see a rainbow of colors.

The colors you see are the visible part of the spectrum of our nearest star, the Sun. Astronomers can investigate a star by studying its spectrum.

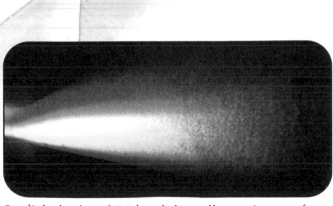

Sunlight looks white but it is really a mixture of colors.

185

16. Lives of the stars

Stars don't last forever. Like us, they are born, grow old and die. In early times, people didn't know about the stages of a star's life. Even so, they told stories about a Sky World where Star People lived and died.

Thousands of stars are being born in this region called the 30 Doradus Nebula.

Star people

The Mi'kmaq people of eastern Canada tell this legend.

One warm, clear night, two sisters lay on their fur sleeping robes under the stars.

"I wish I could marry that small, red star," said Younger Sister.

"I'd choose that gorgeous white one," replied Older Sister. "He's so bright and shiny." Soon both sisters were fast asleep.

Younger Sister awoke with a jolt. A little old man with red eyes was standing beside her. Frightened, she poked her sister.

"What's the matter?" asked Older Sister groggily. Then she gasped. Beside her stood a handsome young man with shining eyes.

"We are going hunting now," said the young man. "Take care of the camp and gather firewood. But do not lift that flat rock by the big tree."

As soon as the two men were gone, Younger Sister ran to the flat rock. She lifted it, stared into the hole below and screamed. Older Sister came running.

Both sisters stared into the hole. Far, far below they could see forests, lakes and rivers.

"We are in the Sky World," Older Sister said in amazement.

"Then those two men must be our Star Husbands," said Younger Sister. "Our wishes have come true!"

How do stars begin?

Stars form out of clouds of gas and dust particles in space. As the particles swirl around, some of them clump together. More and more particles join the clump. Then, under the force of its own gravity, the clump begins to shrink inward. Intense pressure makes the core of the star hotter and hotter. Finally, it becomes hot enough to set off constant nuclear reactions. A star has been born.

What is a nebula?

Any cloud of gas and dust in space is called a nebula. Many nebulae are called "star nurseries" because new stars form from their gases. Some nebulae glow with the light of stars within them. Others are dark and block our view of the stars behind them. The Eagle Nebula, for example, includes the dense pillars of gas and dust shown in the photo below.

Try It!

Explore Orion

1 Find the constellation Orion in the sky. Look for his belt of three bright stars in a straight line.

2 Find Betelgeuse, a red supergiant star in Orion's shoulder. Betelgeuse is 1100 light-years away from Earth.

3 Look for Rigel, a blue supergiant star, on Orion's knee. Rigel is also about 1400 light-years from us.

4 With your binoculars, take a close look at the hazy-looking "star" near the tip of Orion's sword. This bright patch is actually the Orion nebula, a gigantic cloud in which new stars are being born. Though the nebula looks small, it is about 16 light-years across.

In the southern hemisphere, Orion appears to be hanging upside down.

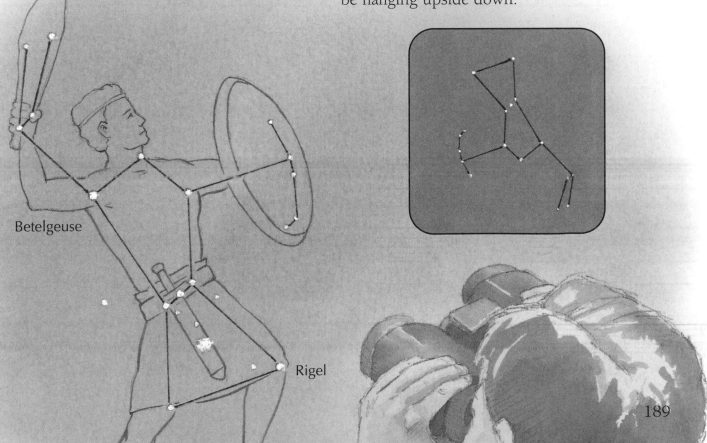

Betelgeuse

Rigel

189

How do stars grow old?

A star spends most of its life glowing steadily. During this time, it uses hydrogen for fuel. Then, after billions of years, the hydrogen in its core runs low. That's when the star enters old age. It begins to burn the hydrogen in the shell around the core. This change makes the star expand and change color. From a midsized yellow or white star, it grows into a red giant.

This star cluster contains a mixture of young white and yellow stars and older red giants.

How do stars die?

After it becomes an elderly red giant, a star continues to change. It may expand and contract as it builds up and loses outer layers of glowing gases. Finally, the old star blasts off all its red-hot gases. It collapses into a small star called a white dwarf. White dwarf stars are usually about the size of the Earth. Because they are so dense, they're very heavy. A white dwarf the size of Earth would weigh as much as the Sun.

When will the Sun die?

The Sun is a middle-aged star. It will probably shine brightly for about 5 billion more years. After that, it will swell into a red giant and finally die as a white dwarf.

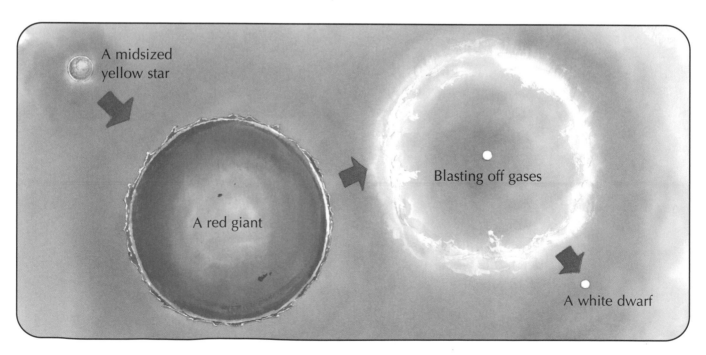

A midsized yellow star

A red giant

Blasting off gases

A white dwarf

What is a supernova?

A supernova is the final explosion of a dying supergiant star. After the main part of its life is over, a really huge star (like Rigel or Betelgeuse) expands into a supergiant. Then, under the force of its own powerful gravity, it begins to collapse. It collapses so quickly that it explodes in a tremendous burst of light. One supernova can be brighter than a whole galaxy.

What is a black hole?

A black hole is a huge amount of matter and energy squished into a small place. Because a black hole is so dense, its gravity is incredibly strong. Nothing — not even light — can escape its pull. Some black holes form when the very largest, brightest stars collapse at the end of their lives. Other black holes are found at the centers of galaxies.

When ancient stars exploded, bits of star material shot out into the universe. Some of it swirled into a cloud of particles that eventually formed our Sun and its planets, including Earth. Everything on Earth — trees, tigers, mountains and people — has been formed from that original stardust. You could say, you're a star!

STAR FACTS

- Mira, a star in the constellation Cetus, appears to grow bright, fade and grow bright again every few months. This happens because Mira is expanding and contracting in its old age.

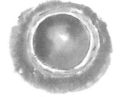

- Canadian astronomer Ian Shelton spotted a bright supernova in 1987. The last time anyone had seen one like it was in 1604.

- The Pleiades, or Seven Sisters, is a cluster of bright young stars in the constellation Taurus. These stars were "born" about 70 million years ago, when the last dinosaurs roamed the Earth.

17. Cities of stars: Galaxies and beyond

On a clear, dark night, far from city lights, look for a pale band of light stretching across the sky. It is the Milky Way galaxy, home to millions of stars including our Sun. But ancient people invented stories to explain this ribbon of light.

Stars of the Milky Way speckle the night sky above a space observatory in Chile. An antenna dish shows an upside-down reflection of the sunset on the horizon.

Stories of the Milky Way

The Vikings saw the Milky Way as the road to Valhalla, the home of the gods.

Native North Americans said that the white trail was snow shaken from the back of Grizzly Bear as it climbed its way into the heavens.

In eastern Europe, Estonians told of Lindu, a young goddess who was engaged to the northern lights.

Lindu prepared for the wedding, but her groom never arrived. Lindu still weeps in the heavens with her white bridal veil drifting across the sky.

In China, people told of a young weaver who married a cowherd. One day the weaver was called back into the heavens by her uncle, the Yellow Emperor. Her desperate young husband tried to follow her but was stopped by a wide white river. The cowherd and the weaver are two bright stars in the summer sky. They still gaze at each other across the river of brightness we call the Milky Way.

What is a galaxy?

A galaxy is a vast collection of stars. Galaxies also contain gas and dust, all held together by gravity. Galaxies come in different shapes and sizes. Large galaxies hold billions of stars. Some look like misty blobs, but others have definite shapes that look like hot dogs or pinwheels.

Three of these galaxies are so close to each other that gravitational forces disrupt their structure.

What is the Milky Way?

The Milky Way is the galaxy we live in. It spins through space like a gigantic pinwheel made of stars. Scientists have discovered a black hole at the center of this glowing spiral.

The Milky Way holds about 200 billion stars, including the Sun. If you could see the Milky Way from a distance, our solar system would look like a tiny speck in one of its curving arms. Light from a star on the far side of this vast galaxy would take about 100 000 years to reach Earth.

We Earthlings are moving through space in one of the arms of the Milky Way.

The Milky Way is also the name given to the cloudy band of light we see in the night sky when we look deep into our galaxy.

Try It!

Reveal the secrets of the Milky Way

YOU WILL NEED

- a clear, moonless night
- an open viewing place away from city lights
- binoculars

1 Gaze at the whole sky. Every star you see is part of the Milky Way galaxy. Earth is located in one of the spiral arms of the disk-like galaxy.

2 Find a hazy band of light across the sky. Now you're looking deep into a neighboring arm of the Milky Way, toward the center of the galaxy.

3 Look at the same hazy band with your binoculars. Surprise! It's made up of millions of stars.

How many galaxies are there?

The universe has billions of galaxies. Astronomers once believed that the galaxies were scattered evenly through space, but we now know that they are clumped together in clusters and huge superclusters.

The Milky Way galaxy is part of a cluster of about 30 galaxies that astronomers call the Local Group.

Two spiral galaxies collide, trapping themselves in orbit around each other. Billions of years from now, they will merge into a single, more massive galaxy. Scientists believe that many present-day galaxies, including the Milky Way, were similarly formed.

How big is the universe?

The universe is bigger than anyone can imagine. Astronomers have picked up radio signals from a galaxy 12 billion light-years away. That's incredibly far, but scientists believe the universe goes even farther. Some galaxies might be so far away that their light still hasn't reached us. In fact, many astronomers think that the universe has no edges.

How did the universe begin?

No one knows how the universe first came to be, but scientists have figured out some things about its past. Early on, the universe was incredibly hot, and everything in it was squeezed close together in a space smaller than a grain of sand. Then, about 10 or 15 billion years ago, the universe suddenly expanded and cooled.

Dust and other particles spread rapidly through space. Scientists call this process the Big Bang.

Over millions of years, the spreading particles clumped together, forming galaxies, stars and planets. Even today, these particles continue to spread apart. The universe is still expanding.

Will the universe ever end?

Some astronomers believe that the universe is like an elastic band that can stretch only so far before it starts to pull in again. If this is the case, the universe may shrink back into a tiny point, heat up and then start again with another Big Bang. The whole process would take billions of years.

Most astronomers, on the other hand, think the universe will continue to expand forever. Either way, you should wonder, not worry, about the universe. It's going to be around for a long, long time.

Try It!

Blow a bubble map of the universe

YOU WILL NEED

- an empty yogurt container
- 125 mL (1/2 c.) liquid dishwashing soap
- 15 mL (1 tbsp.) powder paint
- a spoon
- a straw
- a large sheet of paper

1 Pour the dishwashing soap into the yogurt container. Add the powder paint. Mix well.

2 Blow through the straw into the soap mixture. Keep blowing until the bubbles rise above the top of the container.

3 Lightly lower the paper onto the bubbles. Do not press down.

4 Remove the paper and look at the pattern. Imagine that each line holds thousands of galaxies. That's billions of stars!

This map shows the pattern formed by 1065 galaxies in one small slice of the universe.

18. Discovering the universe

Next time you're walking on a sandy beach, think of this: the universe holds more stars than there are grains of sand on all the world's beaches.

Astronauts on the International Space Station conduct science experiments to learn how people can live in space for months at a time.

Will people ever travel to the stars?

After the Sun, the nearest star to Earth is Proxima Centauri. It is 40 trillion km (25 trillion mi.) away. In a modern spacecraft, the journey to Proxima Centauri would take more than 50 000 years.

Other stars are hundreds and thousands of times farther away. Even if you could somehow travel at the speed of light, a trip to one of them would take many lifetimes. Right now, star travel happens only in science-fiction books and movies. Still, future technology might make this fantasy come true.

What is the best way to explore space?

Human space travel is exciting. It's also dangerous and expensive. That's why many people feel we should concentrate on other ways of learning about space. With powerful telescopes, far-reaching space probes and remote-controlled robots, such as the Mars Exploration Rovers, we can make amazing discoveries without leaving Earth. What do you think? Should we send more people out to explore space?

A golf-cart sized Rover explores the planet Mars. By breaking open rocks, taking photos and sampling soil, Rovers have revealed many signs that water once flowed on the Red Planet.

Will people ever live in space?

Astronauts have already lived on space stations for several months at a time. Scientists are now working on plans for a Moon colony, though it may not be built for a long time. People also dream of living on Mars. Some even suggest changing the Martian environment to make it more like that of Earth. While these ideas seem like science fiction now, some may come true in your lifetime.

What space mysteries remain?

Many questions about space are still unanswered. What is Pluto like? Does life exist on other planets? How many galaxies are there? Will the universe continue to expand forever? Some of these space mysteries may soon be solved. Others will never be explained. Like the people of long ago, we stare at the sky and wonder, "What's out there?"

Answers

Page 77

Space Challenge: How much would you weigh on the Moon?

Answer: To find your weight on the Moon, divide your Earth weight by six.

Page 120

In 1976, a space probe tested soil samples from Mars. Scientists were looking for a long, slow reaction. The space probe tests showed no signs of life. What did your test find?

Answer: The yeast in glass 3 is a living organism. It feeds on sugar and produces bubbles of carbon dioxide gas.

Page 134

Al the Alien sent you postcards from his tour of the solar system. Trouble is, Al forgot to tell you which planet was which. Can you figure it out?

Answer: 1. Mars, 2. Jupiter, 3. Uranus, 4. Mercury, 5. Venus, 6. Saturn, 7. Earth.

Page 142

Comet Challenge: Can you tell from a comet's photo which way the comet is going?

Answer: No, you can't tell from a photo which way a comet is going. The comet's tail always points away from the Sun, so it doesn't always travel behind the comet.

Page 148

Comet Challenge: Why do we see so many craters on the Moon and so few on Earth?

Answer: Craters on Earth are worn away by wind, rain and snow. Because the Moon has no weather, its craters last for millions of years.

Glossary

absorb: to soak up

asteroid: a rocky object orbiting the Sun, much smaller than a planet

astronaut: a person trained to travel in a spacecraft

astronomer: someone who studies the stars, planets and other objects in space

astronomical unit (AU): the average distance from the Earth to the Sun, about 150 million km (93 million mi.)

atmosphere: a layer of gases surrounding a planet

axis: an imaginary line around which a planet spins

Big Bang: the sudden expansion of the early universe from a tiny, hot lump of matter

binary stars: pairs of stars held together by gravity

binoculars: an instrument that helps you see faraway objects more clearly

black hole: an extremely dense object with gravity so strong it traps everything nearby, including light

coma: a huge cloud of gas and dust surrounding the nucleus of a comet

comet: a ball of ice and dust that orbits the Sun

concave: curving inward. The inside of a bowl is concave.

constellation: a group of stars that can be seen as a pattern or picture in the sky

continent: a major landmass

convex: curving outward. The outside of a bowl is convex.

core: the innermost part of a planet, moon or star

corona: the glowing layer of gas around the Sun

crater: a round hole made by a collision with a meteorite, asteroid or comet, or by the collapse of a volcano

crust: the outer covering of a planet or moon

digital: in short, separate pulses

dwarf planet: a round object that orbits the Sun. A dwarf planet has neighbors in its path around the Sun.

earthquake: a sudden jolt that shakes the ground

eclipse: a darkening of the Sun or Moon

equator: the imaginary line that goes around the middle of the Earth

equinox: the first day of spring or fall. On these days the Sun is exactly above the equator and day and night are both 12 hours long.

fireball: an extra-bright and long-lasting meteor

galaxy: a vast collection of stars, gas and dust held together by gravity. Earth is in the Milky Way galaxy.

gas: a form of matter made up of tiny particles that are not connected to one another and so can move freely in space. Air is made up of gases.

geyser: gas or liquid spurting up from the surface of a planet or moon

gravity: an invisible force that pulls objects in the universe toward one another. Gravity holds everything on Earth, keeps the Moon circling the Earth and holds the Earth and planets around the Sun.

hemisphere: half of the Earth's surface. North America is in the northern hemisphere.

hurricane: a violent wind storm

infrared radiation: a form of light energy we can't see

lava: melted rock above ground, usually coming from volcanoes

light-year: the distance light travels in one year

lunar: of the Moon

lunar eclipse: takes place when the Sun, Moon and Earth are in a direct line, with the Earth in the middle. Earth casts a shadow on the Moon and the Moon seems to turn dark.

magma: melted rock inside the Earth

magnitude: the brightness of a star or other object in space

mantle: Earth's middle layer

mass: the amount of matter in an object

meteor: the flash of light produced by a piece of rock or dust falling through Earth's atmosphere

meteorite: a piece of space rock that crashes on the surface of a planet or moon

meteoroid: a piece of dust or rock in space

micrometeorite: a tiny space particle that floats down to Earth's surface.

Milky Way: the galaxy in which we live; also, the hazy band of light our galaxy forms in the night sky

moon: a small planetlike body that circles a planet or asteroid

nebula: a cloud of gas and dust in space

NASA: the National Aeronautics and Space Administration

nucleus: the central core of a comet or other object

observatory: a place with telescopes and other instruments for studying space

orbit: the circular path an object takes through space. Earth orbits around the Sun. Planets, comets and asteroids all have orbits.

oxygen: a gas we need to breathe

phase: the different shapes of the Moon we see as the Moon circles Earth. The Full Moon is a phase of the Moon.

planet: a large round object that orbits the Sun. A planet has no neighbors in its path around the Sun.

radio waves: an invisible form of energy, often emitted by stars

rainbow: a band of color you can see in the sky opposite the Sun, especially after there has been rain

red giant: an old star that has grown to many times its original size

reflect: to bounce light waves back in the direction they came from. Objects can also reflect heat and sound

refract: to bend light waves

revolution: a planet's motion around the Sun

rocket: a machine propelled by the explosions of burning fuel inside it

rotation: the spinning of a planet on its axis

satellite: an object that orbits a larger object in space. The Moon is Earth's natural satellite. A space station is an artificial satellite.

scientist: a person who studies science

shooting star: another name for a meteor

solar: of the Sun

solar eclipse: takes place when the Sun, Moon and Earth are in a direct line with the Moon in the middle. The Moon blocks the light of the Sun and the Sun seems to turn dark.

solar system: the Sun, its planets and their moons, plus smaller orbiting bodies such as asteroids and comets

solar wind: charged particles streaming away from the Sun

solstice: one of the two times of the year when the Sun is farthest from the Earth's equator

spacecraft: a vehicle that can travel beyond Earth's atmosphere

spaceship: a spacecraft that is large enough to carry people

space probe: a robotic spacecraft with no crew

space shuttle: a reusable spacecraft

space station: an orbiting space laboratory where astronauts work and live for weeks or months at a time

spectrum: the pattern formed when starlight is split

star: a glowing ball of superhot gases

supergiant: a very large, very bright star

supernova: the brilliant final explosion of a dying supergiant star

tectonic plates: slabs of Earth's crust

telescope: an instrument that makes very faraway objects seem nearer. Telescopes are often used to look at planets, moons, stars, comets and asteroids.

tide: the regular rise and fall of water in large lakes, oceans and seas. Tides are caused by the pull of the Moon on Earth.

universe: everything that exists, including billions of galaxies

volcano: a place where magma spurts through Earth's crust

weightlessness: when objects and people float freely in space

white dwarf: the small, dense star left behind when a red giant loses its outer layers

Index